#NO FILTER NEEDED

CAMILLA J COLLINS

Published by Goldcrest Books International Ltd
www.goldcrestbooks.com
publish@goldcrestbooks.com

ISBN: 978-1-911505-72-3
eISBN: 978-1-911505-73-0

For my best friend Antonia,

Thank you for being such a wonderful mate to my soul.

You have shaped me into who I am today and I will continue to mould myself to my memories of you.

I will always be dancing with you.

x

"Monday is for taking care of business"
Antonia Yehia

By buying this book you are helping me raise funds for
The Girls' Network

The Girls' Network aims to inspire and empower girls aged 14–19 from the least advantaged communities by connecting them to a mentor and a network of professional role models who are women.

They believe that no girl's future should be limited by her background, gender or parental income. They reach girls via relationships with schools in London, Sussex, Portsmouth, the West Midlands, Greater Manchester, the North East and Liverpool City Region, and support over 1000 girls each year. Volunteer mentors are trained by The Girls' Network and meet their mentees at least once a month for a year. Mentoring is a journey, helping mentees get from where they are to where they want to be.

At the end of the mentoring journey, mentees become ambassadors of The Girls' Network: a free lifelong membership enabling them to continue accessing support and opportunities, and offering them a platform to have their voice heard. The Girls' Network hopes ambassadors will return as mentors once they've entered the world of work, helping them create a self-sustaining social movement with the goal of achieving unlimited futures for all young women. To find out more, visit www.thegirlsnetwork.org.uk.

CONTENTS

INTRODUCTION

I've been wanting to write a book for some time, however, my mind had other ideas. I went into sheer panic each time I thought of trying to create an *entire* book with all its organisation and structure, particularly as I lived my life flying by the seat of my pants and could barely organise myself!

Thankfully, things changed for me and I got my arse in gear and put fingers to keyboard regularly over several months. Across the coming pages are things that I've learnt and tools I've developed over many, many years to help me navigate this thing called life in the most exciting and joyous way possible. Reaping all the joy out of life is an art form that I'm still mastering, but I've learnt to enjoy the ride.

I'm pretty free-spirited but I came to the conclusion that by knuckling down and getting some of this stuff out of my head, I would at least free up some space for more nuggets of wisdom to be stored. My gut was also telling me that perhaps these ideas that I think are awesome, someone else might find awesome too.

So, who is this book for? Well, this book is really for anyone feeling a lot like I did a few years back – a little lost, struggling to recognise their identity and feeling overwhelmed with the pressure to look and be a certain way.

I'm all for positive thinking, however, this book isn't going to be all 'peachy' the entire time because that's not realistic, and I don't see the point in calling a spade anything other than a spade. Even though the truth hurts sometimes, we need to hear it. When things are called out into the open then they are a lot easier to deal with and move on from.

This book in your hands is designed to start a conversation, particularly one with yourself. I'm in no place to tell you what to do; in fact no one is ever in a place to tell you what to do other than yourself. I'm merely making some suggestions, serving up some ideas, and hopefully planting some seeds that, you never know, may produce some powerful trees over time, or at least a pretty garden.

Interspersed in the coming pages are parts of my story, parts of others' and a bit of bullshit busting. I'll be dishing out the occasional fact or figure but really it's all suggestions – you are free to take that which you relate to and leave that which you don't.

I've always found a lot of comfort in identification and I think it's the best form of communication, so I'm hoping there are some parts that resonate with you. But before we delve into the juice of it, I'd just like to say a heartfelt thanks for picking up this book – I admire your curiosity and I'm pretty damn excited to share this with you.

A LITTLE ABOUT ME

My entire life I have played around with my own appearance and for the last 10 years I have been playing with other people's.

WHAT I HAVE LEARNT

Improving your appearance with cosmetics may make you feel better at the time, but it's not a sustainable tool for confidence and happiness in the long run. We are complex creatures and we cannot expect to improve just one area and have all our life problems solved; however, if we try to fix everything all at once we end up feeling overwhelmed, disheartened and ending up at a place far worse off than where we started.

We live in a world that is designed to distract us and which plays on our insecurities left, right, and centre. Society and the media magnify our insecurities so much that we have become dependent on outside influences such as people, places and things to feel worthy.

I may be a hair and make-up artist by trade, but I am also a woman who has struggled with self-confidence and identity over the years. I am human, after all. My own battle has featured eating disorders, addiction, substance abuse and just a general feeling of never fully fitting in.

Growing up, I didn't have trouble making new friends but I never felt like I was truly being myself around them when I did. Whether that was because I felt I couldn't be, or I didn't know how to be, I still don't know and it's something I've struggled to work out throughout my adult life too. I was always trying out new groups of friends 'for size' and I still do to this day. At times I feel frustrated on my lifelong quest to find my 'tribe', but at other times I'm thankful that I never found a group of peers to fully settle down with – if I had stopped my butterfly ways then I wouldn't be able to sit and marvel at the diversity of the people that I have met and who have taught me so much and shaped the person I am today.

I have always been creative; I remember my mother saying that she had never seen me so focussed and inspired as I was when working on my art projects at school. Losing myself in creativity is still my little haven today.

I was a lover of drama and theatre studies at school, which I suppose makes a lot of sense seeing as even when I was off stage I spent a lot of time acting to navigate the people around me – perhaps an early indicator of co-dependency issues and a sign of my addictive tendencies that would rear their ugly heads later on.

After my A-levels it was a toss-up between pursuing art or drama, and as I feared I wasn't thick-skinned enough for drama school, I settled for art school.

Fortunately, I had a wonderful art teacher at school, Mr Ross; he nurtured my ideas and supported and guided me through all my projects over the years. He was the kind of teacher that made you feel like anything was possible, and if all my future days could be spent dreaming, exploring and creating like I did in my art classes, then I was sold. Unfortunately, when I arrived at Central Saint Martins I was in for a reality check, and I quickly discovered that I had just got lucky with Mr Ross's guidance over the last few years.

I completed my first-year foundation there and started a degree, but just one term in I couldn't bear it anymore. After dropping out of Central Saint Martins University at the start of my degree, I was pretty damn lost to say the least and had no idea what I was going to do with my life. Back then it felt like everyone else had it all figured out, in fact, it felt that way for many years until I finally came to the realisation that none of us have it figured out, and we never will. I've now learnt that the joy is in the journey.

After such a miserable time at university I didn't want to go near anything creative again. I threw the baby out with the bathwater and sought out office admin jobs where I thought there would be structure and order. During my long job hunt I was further derailing, I was seeking out security in all the wrong people, places and things. When I finally did land a job, and another after the first one went tits-up, I was not in a good place at all. Having been living so far from my truth for so long, the whole sorry experience of office work lasted about a year. I ended up at The Priory's rehabilitation centre for substance abuse and depression just after my twenty-first birthday, and I spent Christmas and New Year there.

After coming out and taking a few months to rebuild myself, I finally began to get some moments of clarity. I sat down and had a long hard think about who I was, or at least who I wanted to be. I finally allowed myself to dream a little again, and I thought back to my art projects from school that gave me so much enjoyment to work on. Even back then I was exploring the issues from society and the media's ideals, and in doing so I was distorting bodies and faces in many different ways through my art based creations. With the nature of my past artwork in mind, prosthetic make-up seemed like the natural career choice for me.

I had a blast at Greasepaint Make-up School; it was intense, but I loved every minute of it and couldn't wait to go in every day and see what we were learning next. I was in absolute awe of what make-up could do and the transformations I could make through beauty-style applications, but more so through the use of prosthetics. It really opened up my mind to the possibilities and helped my imagination to grow – I was, after all, changing physical, living and breathing things right before my own eyes – it seemed that anything was possible and it was the best feeling as positivity infiltrated into all areas of my life. I started dreaming again and had big hopes for my future. It was certainly my ticket out of the rut that I had been in for so long, and I couldn't wait to share my skills with the world and show them what was possible – make-up artistry to me felt a lot like magic.

When I graduated I started off in the film industry working on shorts, features, commercials and also building my portfolio with collaborative photo shoots as well as assisting make-up artists on their editorial shoots to gain experience. A budding make-up artist would be looking at working for two to three years for free, or expenses only, until they got their foot in the door. For the first year or so I was loving it, but decent jobs were few and far between. It was difficult to find the right work on projects that would elevate me to the next level and help me grow, and I struggled to extend my network to the right people who could push me up the ladder, so to speak. I was working behind the desk at my brother's gym to get a bit of money in, but even he soon got fed up with my constant cancelling and moving of shifts when directors or photographers let me down by cancelling or postponing shoots. My own patience soon started wearing thin, with it all becoming quite the slog and rather unenjoyable. I spent most of my time glued to the computer, refreshing filming industry job boards, applying to work on collaborative shoots, constantly researching and firing off emails to agents for assisting work, and calling up whoever I could. I eventually left the gym and took on the management of a dog walking business, which was flexible enough for me to work my makeup artistry around. During that time I began assisting regularly at weddings, and I just absolutely loved working on them. First, I was being paid for my work, which made me feel far more valued, but most importantly, none of it felt like work at all; I simply felt as if I was just hanging out with the girls on a Saturday morning, having fun with them and making them look and feel a million dollars. The dog walking business was great for me; it provided me with flexibility and a great income, so I could focus on my hair and make-up artistry. I singlehandedly covered just under a year's maternity leave for the owner of the business, and co-ordinated all our clients and walkers each day. It was quite the responsibility however, and there was a fair bit of firefighting, so with my own hair and make-up business picking up pace, I knew I couldn't take on that amount of responsibility again without my make-up career suffering, so when I was asked to cover maternity again for baby number two, I was pushed into the decision to take the plunge and go full-time with hair and make-up, and just somehow make it work!

It took 10 years of building my career in a rather fickle industry, and perhaps the natural process of growing up too, to finally realise I had been paying far too much attention to the wrong things and overcomplicating stuff the whole time.

The last few years have had me in a rather frustrating and painful place and I have felt torn. I love working with people, I love being creative and I love problem solving. My work as a hairstylist and make-up artist allows me to do all those things and I would struggle to find a better alternative career out there for me. But in building my business and agency over the years, I have moulded myself to others' wants and found myself pretending to stand for things that I don't in order to get along in life, which has not served me well in the long run. Living a lie isn't sustainable and the spiritual unrest it causes each day is painful.

A few years ago, just like after art school, I was once again considering throwing the baby out with the bath water and jumping ship from beauty and make-up artistry altogether. I'd grown tired of it all, but from my past experience I knew that every ship has its problems so it was only going to be a matter of time before I was back at the same place again wherever I ended up. At this point I felt I had no choice but to stage an intervention with myself instead of running away. It was time to do the damn work – get stuck in, dig deep and get to the bottom of this mess. I needed to untangle the web of false beliefs and negative thought processes I had created for myself over the years and find out who I really was, what I stood for and how I was going to add value to the world in a way that only I could.

I read, I researched, I listened, I wrote, I spoke and I challenged myself. I looked at my environment, I looked at my friends, I stopped drinking alcohol, I started drinking alcohol, I stopped eating certain foods, I ate those foods again, I started paying attention to how all the seemingly inconsequential things were affecting my mind, and affecting my body. I created a game of it and I began getting to know myself better and better. I learnt to say no to the people, places and things that I knew wouldn't serve me, and yes to the things that might, and a new air of natural confidence started growing within me. I didn't care if others liked it or not, because I now knew my happiness was far more important than their approval in the long run. And soon enough, things just started to slot into place, life started flowing and I found confidence and self-assurance in my days that I never thought I'd have. It felt like I had just woken up.

Now, don't get me wrong, not every day is a bed of roses, it can't be, otherwise it would end up boring and samey.

Life needs its ups and downs and I am human so I can easily fall back into old habits if I'm not keeping a close eye on myself but now I have the knowledge to recognise when I do, and a few tools up my sleeve for getting myself back on track again as quickly as possible.

On reflection, I can see how I spent so many years trundling along in a zombie-like state, fixing on this and that to distract myself from the uncomfortable prospect of wanting to go against the grain. I was following, I was being influenced and very rarely did I stop to ask myself: 'Is this what I actually want?'

I just went with the flow, I people-pleased, did what others expected and got hooked on the instant gratification it gave me. When a spark of my truth did come to the surface, or I felt it in my gut, I denied it with multiple distractions from spin classes, busy-ness, alcohol, food, purchases, hair re-styles, make-up, fashion, etc.

Nowadays, we are conditioned to believe that a large part of our worth is dependent on how we portray ourselves from the outside, and not the contribution we are able to give to the world from our powerful minds and souls on the inside. We end up battling daily with who we actually are and who we think we should be, which is why we wind up feeling so unsure of ourselves. The game of life requires us to constantly adapt ourselves to move forwards, and we need others' approval to get ahead, which is why it's so easy to end up struggling to remember who we actually are, or recognise the person that we are putting out there on a daily basis.

In my industry in particular, I have noticed a rather frightening pattern emerging, where heavy contouring and trending make-up tutorials are producing 'cookie-cutter' results for women all over the world.

This is just one of the many ways that individuality is getting lost, as women strive to recreate the perfect bone structure and enhance their features beyond recognition. And while this all starts out as play, and what we believe to be an innocent confidence booster, it isn't long before we find ourselves swept up by it all, lost in the pursuit of perfection and reliant on cosmetic products, gym regimes, aesthetic practitioners and in some cases, plastic surgeons to go about our daily lives, and feel confident in doing so.

Having become accustomed to being guided through our childhood by our peers, parents and teachers, when their feedback dissipated, it was only natural for us to turn to other sources for guidance on how we should be living and designing our lives, and the media was right there for us when we needed it, and having paid attention to the media's ideals for so long, we have lost touch with the unique qualities that make us individually awesome.

The good news is that everything you are, and everything you'll ever need, is right inside of you. It cannot be permanently lost or removed, so it's just a case of finding it again, which will take some doing. I'm not going to lie. It may not be an easy journey, or a short one, but it's a journey that you're going to have to take if you want to get back to your happy place, or perhaps even discover it for the first time. Most importantly, it's a journey worth taking.

It's going to require you to dig deep, ask yourself a lot of questions, and go back to basics to strip away all the 'fluff' you've accumulated over the years, and shake up your beliefs to find out if they are true or false.

We need to wake up and start seeing everything for what it really is, and most importantly, seeing ourselves and all the greatness within us. This is what this book is designed to do.

What we put into our bodies has a direct impact on what comes out; by not first looking at the physical and non-physical things that we are fuelling our minds and bodies with, and instead seeking only to apply 'dressings' to our exterior, we will never fix the underlying issues – it's like rocking on a rocking chair – it gives you something to do, but it gets you nowhere.

We should not be hiding anything about ourselves, we should not be trying to change what we've been given, we should be capitalising on every single one of our unique qualities, inside and out, and learning to love every part of ourselves. Only then can we be truly confident and happy.

When you wake yourself up to the real pressure that society and the media is putting on you, and you decide to take a good look at yourself and your life, the source of many of your frustrations will become so clear. The solutions that then present themselves, as if by magic, will be far easier to put in place than you could have ever imagined. Rather than having to gain or learn anything new it's a far simpler job of stripping things back.

So, without further ado, let's start breaking it down, remove the filters and get stuck into some transformative work to get you back to you.

COSMETICS OVER THE YEARS

A LITTLE HISTORY LESSON

The notion of beauty is present in almost every society on earth, and the history of cosmetics spans over 7,000 years. Cosmetics and skincare products have come a long way from the days where castor oil was used as a protective balm, and beeswax, olive oil and rosewater were used as skin creams.

So, I thought I'd kick things off with a little history lesson – after all, the beginning is generally a good place to start.

People have always altered their appearance to enhance their status or disguise themselves. From around 3000 BC, Chinese people began to stain their fingernails with gelatin, beeswax and egg white. They used the colours that they wore as a representation of social class. The royals started out by wearing gold and silver, and then later they wore black or red. The lower classes were forbidden to wear bright colours at all on their nails.

Some native tribes painted their faces for ceremonial events and battle, and the same was used by the Aboriginals in Australia.

The geishas in Japan wore lipstick made of crushed safflower petals, and used this to paint their eyebrows and edges of their eyes too. Rice powder was also used to colour the face and back, and a rouge was used to define their noses and contour their eye sockets.

We all want a tan these days; it makes us feel healthier, slimmer and we feel it gives us a radiant glow, but not that long ago, tanned skin was an indication you were from a lower class. From the Renaissance right up until the twentieth century the lower classes had to work outside, and their skin would be darkened from exposure to the sun during agricultural work. Pale skin then was associated with wealth as it meant that you had more leisure time to spend indoors. In stark contrast to today's high demand for fake tan products, white lead paint was actually used to lighten the skin to indicate a higher status and was used by Queen Elizabeth I of England for her look known as *The Mask of Youth*.

In the early 1900s, cosmetics were so unpopular that they could not be bought in department stores, only in theatrical costume stores. Make-up at this time was really only used by prostitutes, performers in cabarets, or those appearing on the black-and-white screen.

The make-up routine back then was extremely basic and only really consisted of a powdered paper to whiten the nose in winter, or an oil-blotting sheet to shine the cheeks in summer. Rouge was considered provocative so was only seen on 'women of the night', although some women used burnt matchsticks to darken their eyelashes and geranium and poppy petals to stain their lips.

It wasn't until 1910 that make-up started to become popular and fashionable due to the influence of ballet and theatre stars in Europe and the United States. Colour was then introduced in Paris.

The Daily Mirror Beauty Book showed that cosmetics were now acceptable for people to wear, and of course, a bit like today, if the media says it's OK then people start to follow. It still took a while to shift the stigma around wearing make-up however, with men still often seeing rouge as a mark of sex, sin and an admission of ugliness; some of these thought processes are still around today.

It was also around this time that cosmetic tattooing was developed by George Burchett. He was able to tattoo on red lips, eyebrows and rosy blushes, and he also developed a more humble technique of camouflaging scars and creating skin tones for men who had been disfigured and suffered skin damage in the First World War.

Max Factor was the first to open up a professional make-up studio for actors in Los Angeles in 1909, and although the store was initially intended for actors of the stage and screen, ordinary women began flocking there to purchase products for their personal use at home.

During the 1920s and 1930s more make-up manufacturers started establishing themselves, many of which are still around today. Lipsticks were one of the most popular cosmetic purchases at the time, because they were colourful and cheap, and today's lipstick-effect theory suggests that the same drive behind lipstick purchases exists today – more on that theory later.

In the 1920s, cosmetics were influenced by the flapper girl styles that embraced dark, round eyes, red lipstick, red nail polish and tanned skin, which was a trend introduced by Coco Chanel. Dozens of new fake tan products were then created with the adoption of Chanel's latest fashion statement, so that both men and women could achieve the now desirable sun-kissed look. In Asia, however, skin whitening continued to represent their ideal of beauty, and still does today. African Americans also still continued to seek ways to lighten their complexion by using skin bleaching, and even hair straightening, to make them appear whiter.

African American skin tones were not really considered or catered for at first, and make-up shades for black women were very limited, as the cosmetic products that were created for paler skin tones were not effective on darker skin. It wasn't until 1970 that cosmetic companies started producing make-up for darker skin tones, such as powders and foundations that didn't make the skin appear grey and provided a more natural match.

When the Second World War hit during 1939 to 1945, most of the basic ingredients used for cosmetics, such as alcohol and petroleum, were diverted into war supply, which then made cosmetics a lot harder to get. As you can imagine, this made for a huge boom in cosmetic purchases after the war and the clever cosmetic developers cottoned on to this and began preparing. Some decided to up their marketing game by giving their products fantasy names such as 'lantern red' and 'sea coral', and others decided to market themselves as the oldest and most established cosmetic brand to gain trust and increase purchases.

The early commercial mascaras were simply pressed cakes containing soap and pigments, and it's actually the same type of mascara I learnt to use at Greasepaint Makeup School. A brush would be dipped into water and rubbed onto the cake to activate the pigments and create a lather; this would then be stroked onto the lashes.

Altering your appearance soon began to take flight and stepped up a notch with more drastic measures being developed in the form of surgery. Facial configuration and social identity dominated a plastic surgeon's world with facelifts being performed as early as 1920. It wasn't until around the 1960s that it grew in popularity and accessibility, for people to reduce the signs of ageing. Cosmetic surgery was mainly for women in the twentieth century, although some men did undergo surgery to help restructure their face after being disfigured in the Second World War.

In 1962 we saw silicone implants being introduced and in the 1980s there was a big push by the American Society of Plastic Surgeons to increase public awareness around the use of cosmetic surgery. As a result of this push, the physicians were granted the legal right to advertise their procedures in 1982, and so the false advertising began with the optimistic advertisements making out that procedures were simple and hazard-free – they were anything but!

In 1998 more than two million Americans underwent cosmetic procedures with liposuction being the most popular, and breast augmentation, eye surgery, facelifts and chemical peels falling not far behind.

During the 1960s and 1970s, when the feminism movement increased in popularity in the Western world, some women decided to make a statement and go without any cosmetics.

Cosmetic development continued through 1970s and the products being produced started being marketed into two divisions – a natural look for daytime and a more sexualised look for the evening.

Contouring and highlighting the face with eyeshadow cream became popular, and when barefaced fashion started trending, women became more aware of the chemicals in their products and hypo allergenic make-up was marketed for those that were more conscious. Avon eventually introduced the saleswoman, and in fact, the whole cosmetics industry opened up big opportunities for lots of women in business as inventors, manufacturers, distributers and promoters.

Let's fast forward to present day. Gradually, an increasing number of males are using cosmetics to enhance their appearance and facial features, and more and more cosmetic brands are tailoring their products to appeal to men. There has been some controversy over this with some feeling that men who wear make-up are neglecting traditional gender. However, others see it as a positive indication of gender equality – why shouldn't men have the right to enhance their appearance with cosmetics as women do?

You may be surprised to know that the Food and Drug Administration (FDA) does not approve or review cosmetics. Like most industries, cosmetic companies resist regulation by government agencies, and they are actually not required by law to report any injuries resulting from the use of their products. In fact, there are quite a few little loopholes and marketing tactics that the cosmetic industry use, and I've got just the women to dig up some dirt on our trusted cosmetic brands. A little later in this book we'll be having a chat with the lovely Rowena Bernado, a former beauty marketing manager for the big beauty brands, turned truth speaker with her blog 'Beauty and the Bullshit'.

PART 1

CONTROL FREAK

In a world where so many things are out of our control, it's no surprise that when we find something that we can actually control, such as dieting for weight loss or enhancing ourselves with aesthetics and surgery, some of us go full pelt with it and try to manipulate it to our advantage as best we can. But what happens when we lose sight of our advantage? What happens when a healthy motivation for bettering ourselves spirals into an obsessive and compulsive need to prove ourselves?

Without the right knowledge and education, and with the wrong things surrounding us and influencing our thoughts and behaviours, it's very easy to think we're boarding the train to glory when really we've embarked on the fast train to unhappiness, anxiety, and ending up at the far less desirable destinations of eating disorders, body dysmorphia and addiction.

Now, I'm no psychologist or mental health expert, but I know someone that is and she'll be putting her two pennyworth in shortly. However, I've had some personal experience in the matter and while I agree to a certain extent that some people are more susceptible to addiction and mental health disorders than others, I also believe that in this highly influential world that we live in, with such a wide selection of information sources available to us, addiction and control is something that can affect us all.

Many years ago, before we had access to the World Wide Web, we were mainly influenced by the physical things that were immediately surrounding us. With no Internet to carry thoughts and ideas from further afar, our truth was created from the people, places and things that were close by. Of course, stories passed down through generations existed, spirituality was present, and people still had imagination, however, others' thoughts and ideas that really challenged the physical things immediately surrounding us, were few and far between.

Compare this to now and we are able to source any information we desire at the click of a button; via the Internet we have access to a lot of truthful facts, but we also have quick access to a lot of rubbish too, and it's often quite hard to tell the difference. It takes a lot of time and effort to fully research and study a subject to arrive at a sensible conclusion on the matter, but time is something we don't believe we have much of these days and this means we often take a lot of things at face value when we shouldn't. The result? We end up adopting beliefs that simply aren't true.

We'll be delving into the tricks of the media and advertisers later in this book, but for now I want to share some thoughts on this topic from my friend and psychotherapist, Zoe Aston. Her area of expertise is addiction and trauma, but these areas, as you can imagine, encompass a lot and she works with patients on a variety of other things these days.

Zoe and I grew up two roads away from each other; we played in each other's paddling pools in the summer and attended the same pre-school, but somewhere around the age of ten we lost touch and it wasn't until eleven years later that we bumped into each other while I was in rehab. So, I wanted to pull Zoe in for a little chat around the subject of addiction and control, and hear her thoughts on the old nature versus nurture argument.

If I cast my mind back to my school days, I can identify some pretty shocking behaviours that small groups of us partook in. Around the age of 13, eating disorders popped onto my radar and my best friend and I used to support one another in skipping meals or helping each other to throw them up in the toilets if we ate them. My memory on the whole subject is a little hazy, but I remember that when I moved school at 14 it wasn't long until I found another group of friends who were conscious of their weight and appearance too, which helped me to fixate and ramp up my weight loss efforts again.

Laxatives, fat-burning pills and skipping as many meals as possible became a regular thing, and I got some momentum with it. Although never hospitalised, I managed to get my weight far lower than it should have been. I convinced my parents to let me eat my dinner in my room, as I was 'too busy with homework', and I hid the food in plastic bags, sending the empty plates downstairs.

I spent my time trawling the Internet for pro-anorexia websites to gain 'thinspiration'. Sometimes, I would end up at the school medical centre exhausted from lack of food; they would let me sleep, or occasionally, I got sent home from school when I had no energy to do anything. It wasn't long before my parents noticed and my mother booked me in to see a psychiatrist, which of course was of no help at all because I didn't see a problem, and to be perfectly honest, I was far too smug about the fact that I was getting weight-dropping results from my efforts.

Throughout the next 5 years I put a strong emphasis on my appearance; a lot of the girls I hung out with during my teenage years did. Without a doubt I was trying to fit in, I imitated the dress sense and habits of those around me, but I was also learning other ways to present myself and exploring my options, which I enjoyed doing. I played with clothing styles and make-up, going through phases of grunge, glam and even gothic. Around the age of 16, when witchcraft was the latest craze among a small group of us, we used to sit in the toilets at lunchtime and carve pentacles into our arms with scissors. Apparently this was our idea of fun. The pentacle carving specifically didn't last long, however, it opened the door to self-harming for me and this became a tool I used for the next six years when I was feeling low, anxious or depressed.

While these examples may sound extreme, to me it was very much the norm back then, as I surrounded myself with others who behaved in a similar way, and I sourced content online to support my activities. So, I normalised it for myself, and I further normalised my behaviour by surrounding myself with similar people. I believe that my past very much shaped my future, which has become my reality today. I have three nieces under the age of twelve and I watch how their behaviours are being shaped by their environment, both physical and non-physical in the online world, and by their peer group that surrounds them.

So, Zoe, my main question to you is:

CAMILLA:

Had I not been surrounded by the people, places and things that I was during my earlier years, I wonder if I would have ever had any problems with addiction and if, still to this day, be so concerned with my appearance?

ZOE:

The nature/nurture debate is a really interesting one and it's only in the last few years that I think we have come to fully understand the science behind it. Loads of the work I do centres around looking at unhelpful patterns, where they come from and why they have formed the way they have. As a psychotherapist, I believe that if we don't go back and explore the reference point, i.e. the where and why, we get stuck in these patterns. I work hard with my clients to get them to a place where they feel empowered and able to choose to do something differently. From there on out, it's their responsibility.

But the question you ask is a juicy one and I personally have also wondered about it and moved backwards and forwards with it in terms of my own mental health. It was only when I discovered the work of a man called Dr Bert Hellinger that I felt I really understood how everything I know about trauma and the human brain came together.

He talks about unresolved experiences, things I would name as trauma, or adverse life experiences, getting trapped in our DNA, which means more than getting trapped in our body – if it's in our DNA it can travel through generations. Which ultimately means that, if his science is correct, we are born with a felt sense that alerts us to be ready to deal with the experiences of generations past. It might look different on the current generation, but it's the body's way of trying to protect itself, just in case it ever finds itself in a war, famished, abused or feeling suicidal again. As an example, a case of hypervigilance and unregulated anxiety might feel intolerable to someone in our generation and they find ways of coping with it through addiction and eating disorders possibly, but actually it is carried trauma from generations past. The reason it winds up into self-defeating and troublesome behaviours is that we are not actually faced with the same challenges our grandparents or great-grandparents were, so unless we use something outside of ourselves to regulate it, we might live in a constant state of feeling on edge.

When people come into therapy, we look at where these things come from so that we can get an idea of the nature/ nurture of the situation. We try to assess how much of it is trapped in your DNA and how much of it is nurture, i.e. things that have uniquely happened to you – friends, social circles, etc. It's my belief that more often than not, we live under stress, or have trouble with emotional regulation, if we carry trauma, and it's almost a blessing when we come across something that helps ease that and means we don't have to work so emotionally hard to feel OK. So in your case, Camilla, I'd hypothesise that when you discovered that controlling your body weight took the strain off you needing to self-regulate, it was, in many ways, a lifesaver. Your eating disorder may well have felt like a relief to slip into.

I'm really passionate about trauma work, because so many clients I have seen have tumbled through therapist after therapist; doctors, psychiatrists, naturopaths, Reiki healers, and the rest, yet they still have not been prompted to consider what trauma they are carrying that isn't theirs to carry. For some reason, I think due to stigma and fear of offending people, it has not been made public knowledge up until now. Now we have a generation of people who want to heal, and I think it's magical. It's why I decided to start my Instagram account: @yourmentalhealthworkout. There are people desperate to heal, and there is no reason why healing should be exclusive to those who can access therapy and treatment. Everyone deserves a chance; whether they take it is up to them.

CAMILLA:

So, that's interesting, and hearing this feels like a bit of a relief if I'm honest – to know that it's not necessarily all my fault, that perhaps there are deep-rooted survival instincts at play here and not purely my own narcissistic tendencies. So, weight loss or weight gain, on its own, isn't a permanent change to one's physical appearance, nor is clothing oneself, changing one's hairstyle or applying make-up to change the outer appearance – these are all reversible and we can quite easily return to our natural physical identity. But what about when we choose to take more drastic measures? When we go 'under the knife' and permanently change our physical identity? Changing the shape of our nose perhaps, which is on the centre of our face? Reshaping the contours of our face and body, and changing the appearance of our unique bone structure with cosmetic fillers and implants? Mentally, how much damage does this do? And how easy is it to help someone face and address the underlying issues after they've taken such drastic actions and permanently changed their outer appearance?

ZOE:

You know, I think that's a very good question, and I have worked with people who have become addicted to plastic surgery and ended up hating what they've done to themselves. It is incredibly sad.

I think the first step is to consider how much awareness the person has. I say that because the likelihood is that they feel very strongly about changing something, such as their nose, because that part of their body or face has become intrinsically linked to strong emotions they don't know how to process. There might be a level of resentment towards someone, for example, if every time they look in the mirror they are subconsciously plummeted into resentment or shame because they see their father's nose or their mother's chin, then they are probably going to become fixated on changing it as a substitute for working through painful emotions that we all do our best to avoid. On the other hand, if someone's parent is very beautiful, that can induce a sense of never being able to be more attractive than Mum, (which developmentally should be allowed to happen) and that might drive someone to feel the desire to significantly change their appearance.

In therapy we attempt to dissolve the defences and adaptations that lead someone to want to get so far away from who they are. My attempt is always to give them access to their vulnerability, look at what's going on at a deeper level, and give them the opportunity to make a choice that they may not have felt they had in the first place.

CAMILLA:

So really, altering one's appearance through cosmetics isn't necessarily anything to do with beauty but more a way of making a physical change in the hope that it will change things mentally?

ZOE:

It can be both. Having pointed out all the above, I do also feel the need to say that I think that the use of make-up and how we present ourselves physically, is a massive part of self-expression, and I encourage it. It helps us figure out how we want to represent who we are to the world. On the other side of it, I've worked with many young people who so desperately want to fit in that they change who they are by following beauty and fashion trends and never get the chance to find out where they actually belong – note, fitting in and belonging are two different things. It's those of us who take it to extremes that I suspect have unhelpful self-beliefs rooted in trauma, which lead to the desire to look significantly different from our natural appearance.

CAMILLA:

Well, I for one would say that a physical and tangible thing seems a hell of a lot easier to fix than a non-physical and abstract one.

ZOE:

Absolutely. That's why so many of us are lured in by the beauty fads that litter our social media feeds these days. It's much quicker and more instantly gratifying than having to actually take a long, hard look at your insides. On the plus side, sometimes we come across things that really work for us and they can be helpful, but the amount of choice out there can also feel overwhelming to many.

CAMILLA:

Oh gosh yes, the 'quick fixes' can be hard to avoid. There are so many quick-fix solutions being presented to us in every company's marketing efforts, which play on our emotions and insecurities to coax us into a purchase.

So, back on the trauma subject, I can understand how easily linking past mental trauma to a physical feature on your body can be done. I should imagine we do it unknowingly, which then results in the same unresolved trauma appearing in another physical aspect of our bodies after that, and once this is altered then it appears in another and so on, and so forth.

ZOE:

Interestingly, I've done a lot of work with eating disorders and I use an exercise that allows us to consider what trauma the part of the body that is disturbing them holds, and what core beliefs and difficult emotions are stored there. From that conversation clients can often find a bit more compassion for the part of the body they are attacking.

CAMILLA:

So, do you have any advice, exercises or processes perhaps that you'd recommend people to go through to ensure that they are making the right decision when planning to alter their appearance in any way?

ZOE:

I might be biased, but I would always suggest seeing a therapist for a few sessions before making an irreversible decision. They are not going to change your mind if your motive is aligned with your authentic self, but it could change your mind if you become aware that your decision is born out of trauma, shame and self-loathing. If that's the case, you'll need some help working through that before you can make the decision from a wholehearted place. The danger of making decisions out of trauma and shame is that you are still left with trauma and shame afterwards – you'll have to face it at some point.

CAMILLA:

And what if someone chose to not to see a therapist and wanted to try to do a bit of work on themselves instead – do you have any advice to help people bust their own false beliefs on their image and identity?

ZOE:

The best suggestion I can give to people I haven't met is simply to give yourself permission to be interested and curious about yourself, and do it in private. Allow yourself to go there. Be curious and be willing to consider as many things as possible. Self-beliefs only change if they are challenged. Coming up with specific and personal affirmations that challenge negative core beliefs can be really helpful. I usually suggest avoiding the standard, punchy, one-liners and finding something that actually feels as though one day, you might be able to believe it.

SELF DEFINITION

We didn't come into this world hating our bodies and feeling unsure of ourselves, in fact, quite the opposite. When we needed something we didn't keep quiet about it; whether that was feeding, nappy changes or just being held, we ensured that our needs were always met and we screamed the place down until we got what we wanted.

As we grew from babies to toddlers we had no body hang-ups and we didn't care what others thought, we simply did as we felt and felt as we did. We were young and we were free. There was no shame around the fact that we had been parading around Aunty June's garden party with our dress tucked into our knickers, and we were all too happy to strip off and run through the sprinkler naked, thinking only about what would make us happy in that moment and not giving one iota of a care to what other people thought about us.

As we grew up and learnt about the world I believe we began taking on other people's insecurities. We started taking notice and buying into the toxic messages of the people and industries around us, and reflecting these messages on ourselves. We allowed others to shape us in how we should and shouldn't be, and as we moulded ourselves further into others' wants and needs we became reliant on our parents and peers to shape us in our behaviour and appearance. By defining ourselves more and more by what others expected of us, we buried our own wants and needs further and became more and more dependent on others to guide us in living our life and shaping our futures – for better or for worse.

Throughout life we define ourselves many times over through our careers, our relationships and our appearance. The start of any of these new self-defining processes is full of excitement; be it a new job in a new industry, a new boyfriend or girlfriend, or a new workout regime and weight-loss diet. We set out goals and embark on the steps to get there. Our imaginations run wild and we start to build momentum as we change our habits and behaviours to suit our new vocation. The problem with each of these, be it the new job, the new relationship, or the new exercise and diet programme, is that we are reliant on others to show us the way. We cannot advance in our careers unless we do what others ask of us; embarking on a new romantic relationship, and deciding to share more and more of our lives with another person, takes some compromise and change to our daily life and thoughts towards the future; and a change to our exercise regime and diet can completely flip our current lifestyle on its head. This is all great at the beginning, by trying out new things and reaching for new goals, we develop and grow. But more often than not, we can wind up lost and trapped by the new way of life and standards we have set for ourselves. Big life changes require us to throw our all into them and the problem with that is that sometimes we leave very few pieces of our previous selves to pick up again should things not work out. We can end up pushing this false life through year after year with careers that we hate, relationships that make us miserable, and in bodies that we feel trapped in. We end up being imprisoned by the standards that are set out for us from those around us for far longer than necessary, resulting in an unbalanced and dissatisfied life, which self-assurance and confidence cannot thrive in.

'Bending the truth'

According to Mintel's research back in 2012,

> *Confidence is becoming something of a luxury in the current economic climate yet, eight out of ten British women feel more confident when wearing make-up. More than just a lipstick or a cover-up, make-up has become the recession's war paint. In effect women are using make-up to put on a brave face. Sales in the market have continued to grow and will continue to do so for as long as the market delivers the feel good factor even if the economy cannot.*[1]

Fast forward seven years and more women, as well as men, are relying on make-up to enhance their appearance and boost their self-esteem.

---

1. *Mintel Press Office https://www.mintel.com/press-centre/beauty-and-personal-care/all-polished-up-nail-make-up-steals-the-show-in-uk-cosmetics-market*

As a make-up artist, I've seen varying degrees of healthy, and non-healthy, relationships with cosmetics in relation to a person's thoughts on their own appearance. For example, not being able to take your bins out with no make-up on for fear of someone seeing you barefaced, is an unhealthy relationship with make-up. Using make-up, even if it is every day, to enhance your natural appearance I see no sinister problem with – it's all part of dressing up for the day. I don't often see people setting off for work in nothing but their underwear, so making your face look more presentable with a touch of make-up is all part of getting ready for the day ahead.

Just as we choose clothes to complement, enhance our body shape and hide the bits we're not so confident about, when it comes to make-up we can bend the truth a little too.

Now, some people may read this statement as dressing up a lie, but I see it as a playful statement for enhancing, or in some cases magnifying, what is already there; and that can go either way.

I bend the truth all the time with my clients and through my work with make-up, and I bend the truth with myself on a daily basis.

These three words can increase my confidence tenfold, so it's something I don't plan on stopping doing any time soon. I do it with the way I dress, how I style my hair, the make-up I wear, and quite often I'll jazz up the words I speak and even the way I move. Because, by bending the truth each day I actually convince myself of a new reality and let's face it, some days we need one of those – rainy days, hungover days, important meeting days – some days require just a little extra push to remember our awesome capabilities so we can go out there and do our thing!

There are some things that are outside of our control, but one thing we do have control over is how we portray ourselves to the outside world, and when we go through the necessary of enhancing our appearance on the outside, a little bit of transformation magic goes on in the inside.

I can lift myself out of a 'funk' super-quickly with a polished, put together make-up just as I can go from feeling like a lethargic couch potato to chomping at the bit for a vigorous workout by putting on my gym clothes.

Simply put, if I'm not looking my best, then I don't perform at my best, and as I know this, why would I not put a few extra minutes of effort in the morning to ensure I'm set up, or rather dressed up, in the best way possible to get the most out of myself and the day?

Through styling, grooming and non-verbal communication, we can paint any picture we want to, and when done correctly it can really help us move further towards our dreams and goals.

I've always found the characterisation aspect of styling fascinating, and I enjoy playing with appearance – which is a good thing considering I made a career out of it!

A full-on prosthetic make-up is a lot of fun to do and can really transform and produce jaw-dropping results, but I also love to explore subtle changes, such as bringing out someone's natural eye colour with a complementing shadow, or defining their nose shape to change the overall appearance.

After all these years I still find it fascinating how little changes here and there can completely alter not only how we are perceived, but how also how we perceive ourselves. The moments when my clients realise this by watching me at work in the mirror is pure magic, and one of the most rewarding parts of my job.

The impact of imagery has been determined by social psychologists, in that when someone meets you for the first time, a few seconds is all it takes for them to form a whole host of determinations about your character and abilities. In just a few seconds, people form impressions of you based almost entirely on what they see – the clothes you wear, the way your hair is styled, the smile you put on and generally how you carry yourself along with the rest of your nonverbal communications.

When it comes to business nowadays the rigid 'dress for success' rules have changed to give way to more flexible guidelines that encompass casual business looks as well as the more traditional power suits. There are always ways to improve your appearance and a lot of them are unbelievably simple to do. That is why I love it when I get feedback from busy mothers or professionals who say by applying just a fraction of what we'd covered in their lesson, such as grooming their brows or enhancing their bone structure with a little bit of contouring, has completely transformed their moods, enhanced their day, and they're feeling the shift in all areas.

So, while we're on the subject of appearance, and the shifts it can bring to our confidence and demeanour, I've asked my dear friend, style coach and image consultant, Janette Miller, to share her story and some words of wisdom on the topic of personal styling.

As someone who suffered with low self-esteem and lack of confidence growing up, I am so thankful that I now know how quickly I can ooze confidence by wearing certain clothes.

I was the girl who was chosen last for teams in PE at school. I was the one who played by herself when my best friend was off sick, as she was my only friend. I was the one whose mum didn't pack any evening clothes for my first school trip away. I was the one who was compared to family members for having thick hair and wearing glasses.

I believed from a young age that it was easier to blend in and hide if possible.

At age 13 I worked my first job at my dad's ladies' boutique in South West London. Perhaps it was a combination of my place of work and the fact I was growing up, but I started to feel style conscious and I soon began finding my own taste in clothes that I was allowed to wear. I still didn't have many friends, my brother actually remarked that I had lots of nice clothes, but no friends – I guess that translates to 'all dressed up and nowhere to go' in today's language.

When I left school my confidence was beginning to increase, my relationships improved and my circle of friends grew, as I was beginning to own myself. I wasn't suddenly an extrovert; quite the opposite in fact. I remember saying to someone at college that I want to be 'just there' i.e. not stand out or anything. He looked at me, puzzled. I guess most girls at that age wanted to be the centre of attention, but I couldn't think of anything worse.

As an adult, my confidence increased further. I was confident enough to go out there, to get the job, the guy, the house. Life felt good. However, this presented a new problem. My increase in confidence also resulted in backlash from others around me. I came to the conclusion that it was actually easier to blend in, because by not standing out, I didn't run the risk of being the butt of someone's joke. It felt like I was back at school again – I actually went backwards in terms of confidence and retreated, and so I wore clothes to blend in and walk around unnoticed.

This way of being went on for years until I hit breaking point and rebelled; I eventually said to myself, and the world, that 'enough is enough! I want to wear what I want to wear.'

Dressing to please others is exhausting. I no longer care what someone says if I rock up to an event in the most expensive-looking dress. I'm not looking for attention; it's an amazing dress and I want to wear it, for heaven's sake!

Am I what I wear? Yes. I feel confident now, and with this confidence my relationships have improved as I have the self-assurance to go for what I want. I now help to change others' lives by doing the job I love and sharing my experiences.

Through your choice of style you can be whoever you want to be with what you're wearing. If you don't believe this to be true, then look at your favourite actor or actress. They're given a script, they're given a costume, and then get into character. They play out the role that looks like the person they are dressed as. The same applies to fancy dress parties. You get to choose who you will be dressed up as and act like that character for the entire night. How amazing is that?

Our clothes are powerful, but you must remember to maintain a positive self-image. If you don't, your clothes will feel like a costume that you don't want to take off when the party ends. The idea of 'costume' is something you can use to your advantage. Wear the clothes that make you feel good; not just look amazing in, but feel good.

When you look in your wardrobe and say you have nothing to wear, often one of the overlooked reasons is that your clothes no longer reflect the person that you are or desire to be. They were worn by the person you used to be.

Decide who you are and who you want to be. Always be open to style inspiration – it's all around us, even in nature. Act like the person you want to be and don't be afraid to experiment *with clothes that you think may reflect this. Once you get comfortable and good at this, you'll soon find confidence to do the things that attract what you truly want.*

You are what you wear. Make a commitment today to become who you desire to be by wearing the clothes you believe that person would wear.

Janette Miller

SEVEN SECONDS

Did you know that upon first meeting we form an opinion on someone within just a mere seven seconds?

Sociolinguist Albert Mehrabian did a bit of research into communication and discovered that 7% of a verbal message comes from the words used, 38% comes from the vocal tone, pacing and inflexion and a whopping 55% of the message is transmitted by appearance and body language.

Now this chapter of the book is not encouraging you to pretend to be something that you are not, quite the contrary in fact, it is encouraging you to capitalise on everything that you already are.

We may believe we should never judge a book by its cover but evidently we do, which makes first impressions count for everything.

The fact that we have discrimination laws addressing physical appearance such as age, weight and hygiene tells us that first impressions permeate through all areas of society within our professional and personal life.

Our lives are moving at a ridiculously fast pace these days with technology allowing images and messages to swamp us more and more, so we are forced to filter visual cues and messages quickly and end up making snap judgements now more than ever before.

As the saying goes: 'You never get a second chance to make a first impression'. However, each time we encounter the same person again, our impressions are reset. So, if you're coming across the same person more than once then you can actually work on changing and improving those impressions. With this in mind, it's always worth putting the effort in and working on yourself to improve and tailor your impression for your audience to get the desired result. However, where first impressions really count, such as job interviews and first dates, we may never get a second or third encounter, so we really want to make sure we get it right the first time.

When making an impression it's super important to know your audience; however, I believe it's even more important to know yourself better.

You see, the first impression that we make isn't always something that we are solely responsible for.

When we interact with others we factor in a lot of assumptions based on our own past experiences, and this can lead us to make quick judgements that may be untrue.

Has anyone ever told you that, 'you can't tar them with the same brush'? Well, it's a fair point, as by assuming someone is bad news just because something about them reminds you of an unsavoury character in your past is not always the right assumption; it could quite innocently be a physical, facial feature, or a familiar item of clothing, rather than a negative character trait that affects a first impression of someone else. By ruling everyone and everything out as soon as you notice something a little 'off', you can end up going through life being very closed-minded. But on the flip side, if you were to ignore all the signs and alarm bells when they do crop up, you then risk making the same mistakes again and again, and fail to see the pattern that can help you make more effective decisions in the future. So, keeping a relatively open mind, and being aware of your thought processes and questioning your own beliefs regularly, is a healthy habit to get into. Furthermore, it really helps you to feel more secure within yourself and confident in your own decision-making abilities.

Nothing is more empowering than sticking to your guns, knowing that what you're feeling is valid and believing in the person you are and the person that you are putting out there. But sadly so many of us don't.

From an early age we are programmed to get ahead by moulding ourselves to what others want to see in order to get into schools and universities, nail job interviews or navigate the dating world successfully.

We seek others' approval all the time to get on in life, from making friends to finding spouses, or encouraging others to work with us in a professional or personal manner.

When we are confronted with a new person, our views of trust form even faster than attraction, which is likely due to our ingrained survival instincts.

Nothing spells out confidence more than a neutral, relaxed and coherent person. Confidence of this kind we are all drawn to and want to engage with. People like this allow us to connect with them and encourage us to trust them; they are not trying to be something they are not and there is a sense of peace about these people that is attractive.

Overconfidence, on the other hand, is just a huge turn-off and I, as I'm sure you, have come across many people who seem to have absolutely no awareness whatsoever and either come off as rude or desperate. But rarely does overconfidence stem from anything other than a lack of self-worth. Overconfident people are in need of constant admiration and approval from others, because their sense of self-worth is dependent on what others think of them. Behind their façade is unhappiness and a distinct lack of self-belief. I think a lot of us at some time or another have acted out with overconfidence and can empathise with this school of thought. But where did it get us? It's a bit like telling a lie and then having to tell a bunch of other lies just to keep the first one going. It leads you down a pretty miserable path of constantly having to hide your true self to reinforce the impression that you are someone that you're not. This is not a sustainable way to live and it's one of the unhappiest ways to conduct one's life.

The well-established sentiment, 'If a person looks good, they feel good', holds true for most of us, and it works both ways – we feel good in ourselves when we make a bit of effort with our appearance, and we also feel good towards others when it's clear they have made a bit of effort with theirs. This goes beyond the surface though as there is only so much dressing up of a poor lifestyle one can do, and only so long that one can do it for before the cracks begin to show and they becomes exhausted – being something you're not is exhausting work, after all.

We've only got one mind and body, and the stuff that we put it through is mind-boggling when you think about it. If you get a new and expensive handbag, you take pride in it, you're careful not to place it on the floor where it could get dirty and you only take it out on particularly special occasions. The same goes with a new and expensive car; you wouldn't leave it vulnerably parked on a dodgy street overnight, nor would you let the petrol gauge run right down to empty for risk of damaging the engine. You see, when we value things we dedicate a lot more time and effort to ensure they are looked after in all situations and this shows; by the handbag looking as nearly new from being cared for and placed back in its dust bag after each use, or the car keeping its paintwork and alloys intact, with all parts working nicely from regular services and plenty of petrol to sustain it.

So why in God's name do we do not treat ourselves the same way? It's far easier to replace a handbag or a car than to replace parts of ourselves, yet sometimes we place more value on material items than our own mind and bodies. Our bodies are pretty magnificent things when you delve into their workings, and it would not be a waste of your time to have a little look into the science behind your being – mainly because things are a lot easier to operate when you have a manual. When you understand what goes in versus what comes out, then firing on all four cylinders daily will become a lot easier for you to do, in fact it will feel effortless, which is how it should be.

We'll actually be delving into some of this later, but for now just please remind yourself that none of us are superhuman, and eventually something's gotta give. Our bodies can take a lot, and boy do we give them a run for their money with the physical and mental stress we put them through. We should be treating ourselves with the utmost respect and care before anyone else, because we're no good to anyone if we're not here! Just like with an aeroplane emergency landing, we should be securing our own oxygen masks first, at all times. Like the handbag we too should be careful about where we are placing ourselves and the 'dirt' we are likely to pick up from environments we hang around in. We should be selective about where, and with whom, we are spending our time. We can't be everywhere and please all people; if the handbag was out on show every day, it would end up tired-looking very quickly – much like we do when we're burning the candle at both ends. And like the car having regular services, how often do we stop to check in with ourselves to assess if our mind and body are in good working order, or ensure we have enough fuel, and the right fuel at that, so we are not running on empty and damaging our own internal engines? A lot of us don't do any of it as regularly as we should. We push ourselves to the limit and overstretch ourselves by taking on too much, trying to be everywhere, pleasing everyone at work and home, resenting most of it and most likely fuelling our body with either rubbish or not enough along the way.

So yes, I'm saying that if you don't think carefully about your actions and check in with yourself, you're going to end up looking very much like the tired handbag, battered and coming apart at the seams – and no amount of make-up or hairspray can cover that up.

Before you hit burnout and reach for the nearest quick fix being pushed at you by the media – just STOP!

» Look at your diary.

» Look at your workload.

» Look at you.

» Are there things scheduled in your diary that aren't serving you well?

» Are their items on your to-do list that could, or should, be delegated?

» And most importantly, what is your body telling you?

» Look in the mirror at the physical signs: is your skin luminous or washed out? Are your eyes bright or dull? Does what is staring back at you reflect how you feel?

» And now quieten your mind for a while; listen to your internal dialogue. Is it negative or positive? Are you being kind to yourself, or are you putting yourself down?

THE BRAND OF YOU

The only brand you should be invested in is the brand of you.

Just like brands create core values that gain our trust in them, we should also be sticking by our own core values so that not only others can place their trust in us, but we can fully trust in ourselves at all times and conduct our lives in a way that is true to us. In business, when a brand copies another brand, it never lasts; there is no individuality there and the brand has a hard time keeping up the façade, as what they're putting out there just doesn't flow right and people pick up on this very quickly. The same goes for people. If you're grabbing on to others' beliefs, and pretending that you're passionate about them, then people will smell a rat.

I'm not talking about experimenting with new style habits or adopting new fashion trends, but more how you go about your daily business; your thought process and the actions you take each and every day. You can't build the awesome brand of you on other people's values, as somewhere along the line you'll grow tired and will no longer be able to sustain it, not to mention you'll feel pretty uncomfortable as you're acting out of character the whole time.

Every business has a unique selling point (USP) and so do you. Don't borrow someone else's – own your own.

Every day of our lives should be lived with purpose. It's so easy to sit and scroll through social media, staring into others' highlight reels and gaining inspiration on how we should be conducting our own lives. But it's also so easy to overlook the fact that none of it is actually real. In every photo we look at, we're seeing the finished product and are not taking into consideration the work it took to get there, or even what is outside the perfectly cropped box it sits in. It may be social but it's media after all, and every single image is crafted carefully to speak a specific message and tap into a particular emotion within us. So much of our lives are spent online, and even though we are aware of this, it's still so easy to be brainwashed each day by scrolling through the Internet on our phones. Just the other day I was sitting on the Underground and for once I didn't have my head buried in my phone, furiously typing WhatsApp messages or answering emails. As I sat there and looked around the carriage and at the people around me, I realised that the Northern Line did not have a single person on it that resembled the people I had been scrolling past on social media earlier that day. I suddenly I felt an enormous amount of pressure lifted from me and instantly relaxed. I could see the individuality in everyone around me; some with make-up, some without, some in casual clothing and others in smart attire, some looking exhausted and others looking content, and in that moment I was reminded that I'm living in a real world and the real world looks nothing like what I see on Instagram, nor do the people in the real world look like they do on their Facebook profile photos. From this momentary realisation I wondered exactly how long I had been out of touch with reality that day, or perhaps I had been out of it for a couple of days up until that point. The danger of viewing so much of life through the screens of my devices became apparent. Searching online and scrolling through social media as often as I do does nothing for me other than take me away from reality and make me feel inadequate. On that train there were probably far more people that I could speak to and make a genuine connection with than concerning myself with the influence and 'inspo' that the online world is providing me with to alter my appearance, adopt new trends and enhance my life in a way that would mean that very few people in the real world could actually relate or connect to me. I realised that changing myself to suit these fickle standards would, in fact, put me further into isolation within society.

Owning all your flaws, your unique abilities and your 'not so perfect' life is actually so important to connect with everyone around you, as doing anything else places you outside of people's relatability zone.

Personal branding is quite the trend at the moment, but it's not about creating some fictitious brand and changing yourself to suit it, it's about harnessing your identity and unashamedly owning it, as you so rightly should. My dear friend, Hannah Power, is a personal branding specialist and entrepreneur who has a wonderful way of talking sense, and is never afraid to do so, so I asked her to contribute some words of wisdom to this section of the book and here they are:

The world is changing, giving us an opportunity to lead. People are craving authenticity, they're craving real people, they're craving real stories, having a personal brand has never been more important.

There are a variety of things that hold us back when we want to create a brand, and this can often come from a place of fear, which creates excuses. 'It's all been said' 'I haven't got anything to say' 'I'm not good enough' are often things we say to ourselves to convince ourselves that holding back is the right thing for us to do.

It's true everything has been said, and there are loads of people out there, but what makes you unique to your audience is your story; you are a messenger – you have your own audience and your own unique flair. So, by stepping up and stepping into your own personal brand, you are inspiring and leading others.

Your brand is the whole of you; it's your skills and expertise, it's your passion, it's your goals, it's your experience. It's the people that you serve; it's the things you've learnt along the way. Understanding and investing in your personal brand enables opportunity, fulfilment and excitement. By owning who we are and sharing that with others, we become hugely powerful. You are powerful by just being who you are, by sharing your message and sharing your story.

If you aren't sure where to start, start right at the beginning. A personal brand isn't about getting free stuff or sharing photos of salads on Instagram, it's about deeply understanding what your purpose is; what are you here to do? Once you understand this, you can start living this purpose, stepping into the person you truly are.

Mark Twain once said:

"The two most important days in your life are the day you are born and the day you find out why you were born."

Now is your opportunity to discover that why, and start living your truth.

Hannah Power

Ahead of the next chapter, here's a little homework for you. Ask yourself:

» What do you want for yourself?

» How do you want to be seen by others?

» If you walked into a room, what would you want others to think of you?

» Do you want them to think you look beautiful but unapproachable, or do you want them to feel your warmth, energy and self-assurance and be drawn to you?

And just think of this for a minute – if you lived on a desert island, what on your body would actually bother you? When there is no one else there but you, would you be bothered by the things that are bothering you right now? And is your current opinion of yourself based on what others think of you?

Take a few minutes to push life as you know it to one side and dream up the perfect way in which you would like others to see you.

» What would others remark about you? What would be the first thing that they notice about you? Would they notice you are smart? Thin? Stylish? Kind? Generous?

» What would your friends and family say about you in your ideal world? And why are these things important to you?

» Think of specific things that would make you feel worthy. What accomplishments in life have you had, or what accomplishments would you like to have, that are truly important to you? How do you think of yourself, or how will you think of yourself, in relation to accomplishing these things?

Asking ourselves questions is the best way of discovering new things about ourselves, and the right questions can often bring up some surprising answers that we didn't really know on a conscious level.

With all the questions above in mind, and perhaps you've asked yourself some of your own, imagine your ideal self walking into a room and bring up a strong mental picture, and really notice how it feels. How are people responding to you? Do you feel confident? Does it feel good? Do you feel a little full of yourself? If so, good – you should feel full of yourself! And before you think this is in anyway narcissistic, it's not. Narcissism is loving yourself at the *expense* of others. Feeling good, accomplished and self-assured is loving yourself so that you can *contribute* to others. There's a difference!

Hold on to this new image and keep it with you until the end of the book where we will be doing some more self-transforming work with your imagination.

COMPOUND AND RIPPLE

The Compound Effect is a bit of a game changer really. It was brought to my attention by Darren Hardy and it has changed my life! In his book, Darren illustrates how seemingly inconsequential changes can compound over time to create big results.

Consistency is key to producing results of any kind. If you want to increase your fitness levels, or lose ten pounds, then you need to consistently put in the time or effort each week to do the work to get to your goal. Whether that's running a little every day to build your stamina, or cutting out your morning latte and pastry on the way to work. You need to incorporate new changes every single day to eventually see the results. You can't just do one big run and expect your fitness levels to soar, nor can you cut the latte and pastry out for just a couple of days and expect the pounds to drop off. But if you consistently did just fifteen minutes of running each day, then over time you'd see improvement, and by the end of the month you'd see a huge improvement in your capabilities to run for longer and faster. The same principle applies to the latte and pastry, which we'll go through in a bit more detail in a minute.

Achieving results often seems like a lot of work, but in some cases it's the opposite. In the case of the latte and pastry it may seem like you are sacrificing something, but by forgoing the twenty minutes of pleasure that you think it gives you, you actually end up saving far more than the calories; you'll end up saving money, saving time, increasing your energy levels, enhancing your mood and improving your skin. Can you imagine what then happens when you have more time, more money, more energy and feel better about yourself? Well, it infiltrates into all areas of your life as you have more time and energy to get things done, so that then frees you up to spend the money you've saved on the things you enjoy doing or things that you really want. And you feel awesome about it because your skin is looking far better than it was and your confidence has increased as a result. And can you imagine the impact that all this would then have on all areas of your life and the people around you? You'd be a much better person to be around, your relationships with friends and family would improve and you'd being opening new doors for yourself as you attract new people and things into your life. You'd be adding more value to the planet, which would make you feel even better about yourself and so on and so forth – and that's the magic of the compound effect and its wonderful ripples!

Hopefully that illustrates clearly why it's so much more beneficial to put a bit of work in with yourself instead of turning to the many quick fixes available to us these days.

Darren gives lots of examples in his book that really hit home, like the one above, but please allow me to give you one of my own.

Let's go back to the latte and pastry and look at that in some finer detail. That's around 420 calories a day you are consuming purely out of habit, and based on a 5-working-day week, this adds up to 2,100 calories a week. To burn off those calories you would then have to walk around 20 to 25 miles a week. Assuming it takes you around 20 minutes to eat your pastry and sip on your latte, you would actually have to walk for around 2.5 to 3 hours each day to simply burn it off.

'But I'm relatively fit and like to do some running in the week, so I allow myself the treat,' you say. Okay, well with running you'd burn an average of about 300 calories per 30 minutes, which means you'd need to run for about 40 minutes, which is double the amount of time it took you to consume it. You may really enjoy running, but if fat loss is your goal, wouldn't it be nice to have the option to run because you choose to and not because you're forcing yourself to undo a poor decision earlier that morning? Pick your battles, people!

Over to the money side of this particular case: you will spend £24 per week, which is around £96 per month, which equates to £1,152 a year – that's a pretty nice holiday there. But say you don't spend it on a holiday and just keep it to the side – in 5 years you'll save £5,760, and in a further 15 years £23,040, just by cutting out a latte and a pastry 5 days a week on your way to work. What could you do with £23,040? A lot.

These are all just rough figures, of course, as everybody is different, the rate at which we burn calories will differ depending on many factors, but you get the gist. The thing is, we overcomplicate things all the time. Our busy world around us is throwing up distractions every hour of the day and veering us off track from our goals. We are so often reacting to things around us, without really thinking our responses through, and wind up exhausted and reaching for quick fixes and magic pills to solve the issue, which they don't, or if they do then they cost us dearly. If you then work out how many hours you would have to work to earn the money for these magic lotions, potions and pills, you'd soon realise that it's false economy. The chances are that you're creating the problem of bad skin and weight gain by putting so much stress on your mind and body to work so hard in order to afford the 'cures' in the first place.

The ability to lose weight, improve our skin and enhance our appearance is within us all, and it doesn't come from a magic pill or potion. You don't need anything else other than a strategy and consistency – more coming up on that later.

Trust me, everything is so much easier when you break it down, but rarely do we stop to think and work these things out. Most of us see something that we admire and would love to achieve, be it a business milestone, a slender and toned body or luminous and radiant skin, but we immediately write it off as unobtainable because it's so far removed from our current reality. If you just sat down quietly for a few minutes to really think logically about it, you would see that almost any achievement is possible if you break it down into manageable chunks.

If you take that end goal and calmly work backwards from it to figure out the small, manageable steps it would take you to get there, yes there might be a lot of steps, but what you would have is a foolproof blueprint that would deliver your desired result, which means that a lot of things that you think are not possible for you, actually are.

Lots of things we think are out of our reach are possible for all of us, but unfortunately overwhelmingness sets in and un-enthuses us before we've had a chance to think rationally about it.

Taking some time to think about what we really want to aspire to, and then taking the time to break it down and work out how we can get there, will prompt us to change our short-term perceptions and behaviours. By then making consistent efforts to change our short-term behaviours, over time we begin to reprogramme our minds, changing what we link pleasure and pain to, and that leads to long-term change.

THE THREE Ps

There's a saying: 'Where focus goes, energy flows', and there have been periods in my life when I was up against quite a bit of resistance to get tasks done, so much so that I've had to daily chant these five words like a mantra to remind myself of the power of my own thinking, and keep me on the straight and narrow.

I've never been a great one for sitting still physically; I think I lasted about fifteen minutes in a yoga class once, it felt like torture! Calming and stilling my mind is something I try to work on, it's a daily practice and something I'm still in the process of learning to do more effectively. I have good days and bad days with it, just like anything in life, I suppose.

Thankfully, it's not just me and there is a bit of science to back up why my whirring mind can send me into panics over quite ridiculous stuff. Before we take a little look at the human brain and as to why that happens, I first want to talk about the three Ps that are the driving force behind every single human on this planet. Once you've got your Ps in check you gain control and can completely redirect your life, if you want to. The three Ps that I am referring to are Pain, Pleasure and Perception.

Our intellect and emotion are at war most days of the week. Ever wonder why you end up making poor decisions that you know are wrong? It's because at the time you had an emotional response to the decision, and emotion will win over logic every time. Whether it's eating the big slab of cake with vanilla frosting you know you shouldn't have, continuing to develop a relationship with someone you know isn't right for you, or procrastinating and putting off tasks that you know will cause far more stress later in the week when you have to cram them in. In all of these situations there is pain and pleasure linked to your actions, and it's what drives you to make the decisions that you do. Avoiding pain is simply a survival instinct. Getting a grip on yourself isn't about disciplining yourself, it's about understanding what's driving you to think and act the way that you do, and then reprogramming these drivers. In other words, you need to change what your brain associates pain and pleasure with so that you can stop disrupting and sabotaging your own life.

Everything we do is influenced by emotion, and marketers know this. We don't buy the best product anymore; we purchase what we associate the most pleasure and the least pain with. This is why all marketing and advertising efforts are emotive, and they link pleasure to their product while sometimes even linking pain to their competitors. If you want to motivate or influence a human being you need to work out what motivates and influences them, and that means working out their pain-and-pleasure links.

So, we know that every day we can grow our strength and resilience, and enhance all areas of our life by compounding good behaviour, but why is it so damn hard to get the ball rolling? And why do we insist on sabotaging our own good work with one poor decision that can very easily send our results compounding in the wrong direction? I shall tell you.

As we discussed in the previous chapter, it's easy to get momentum with choosing to take positive action and compounding those results over time, but before you can do that, you need to make sure your mind is in check to be able to make those good decisions in the first place. Once you've tipped the balance of your pain-and-pleasure links to a particular action and its perceived outcome, then you can switch your focus and have control of it, which puts you in a much better position for success with anything you're trying to achieve, or any big-ass goals that you're going after.

There is one thing, and only one thing, that stops us from being great, and that is fear. Fear of failure, fear of rejection, even in some cases fear of success. And what happens if you fail or get rejected? You experience pain.

Let's take brushing your teeth, for example. Do you do it because you love the process? No, you do it because you don't want people judging you for having bad breath, or worse, because your teeth will fall out due to lack of care.

The same could be said for applying make-up. For most people it's a chore and they would prefer the extra fifteen minutes in bed in the morning, but wearing make-up makes our lives easier and more pleasurable by not having to spend the day worrying that anyone is judging us and thinking we look like we've made no effort at all. And let's not also forget the power of a very well done make-up that boosts your self-esteem and brings in compliments all day long to hit those pleasure points. As you can see, the driving force for each of these actions is the perception of the pleasure or pain you will get from them after it's done, not while you are doing it. With every decision you make, and action that you take, you are avoiding pain and gaining pleasure each time with its outcome.

Let's look at eating that cake, or chocolate, or anything in fact with sugar in it. You know that it will make you put on weight and you know that if you were to put on weight you would experience pain when your clothes don't fit and you look larger in the mirror. But, before any of that comes the pure pleasure from the taste, and the sugar high of eating it is far more instant and quick to get. If you think rationally about it, then it makes no sense at all to not only sabotage your long-term health and weight-loss efforts for a couple of minutes of pleasure, but to also run the risk of hitting a sugar crash shortly afterwards. This would cause you to crave more sugary foods, which would once again cause you pain to resist, and likely cause you to give in again to gain instant pleasure and start the vicious cycle all over again. Most people don't think about the consequences of their actions, they just jump to the immediate effect – will it give me pleasure or will it give me pain *in this moment?*

We give up so much freedom within our lives through procrastination, because we link more pain to taking action in that moment than pleasure for getting whatever it is done and dusted – it's a completely false economy.

I did a bikini fitness show last year and my goodness was that a lesson in pain-and-pleasure links for me? The whole process helped me to completely reprogramme areas of my mind that are still running well today. I went in for a very hard, seven-week prep for the show when really a fourteen-week prep would have been far better, but I didn't have the time as it was the last show of the season. It was either do it in seven weeks or not do it at all. I linked a lot of pain to the fact that if I waited until next year I would go off the boil and probably end up simply not doing it. So it was the fear of failure and its pain that drove me to knuckle down to it there and then. I had five days to make the decision as to whether I would enter the show, and I had decided on day one that I was going to do it, but I wanted to make doubly sure that I could follow through with it. What I did over the five days before I made it official was mentally prepare myself for what was to come. I got working on those pain-and-pleasure links within my brain each day by imagining all the outcomes and visualising what life would be like with the run-up, and on show day itself, in only positive and pleasurable ways. I linked pleasure to every aspect of the process in my mind; the weight loss, the mental focus from no alcohol, the productivity I would get to achieve more with my business from fewer distractions, the pretty sparkly bikini I'd get to buy and feel comfortable parading on stage in. For every pain point, I linked pleasure to it, and I made this part of my thoughts each day in the five-day lead-up to agreeing to it, which put me in very good stead to kick off the seven-week show preparation on a positive note, and in the right gear for success. Not only did I get up on that stage, love every minute of it and feel proud of my achievements, but also, thanks to getting my pain-and-pleasure links sorted, I enjoyed the entire process – well for the most part.

Giving yourself some quiet time is so important to rationally think and change your perception of things. Most of us spend our lives in reaction instead of in control. When we give ourselves the time to think clearly and rationally, and the space to visualise the favourable outcomes, then we can control where our focus goes and ultimately where our energy then flows.

A lot of our pain links are the products of our false beliefs that we have created from previous situations. Again, this is perception. We perceive things will go well, or badly, based on our previous experience in a similar situation, and this last situation is where our perception was created and our pain-and-pleasure links were formed. For instance, if we were in a wonderful, loving relationship but then we got dumped, we may form a belief that relationships equal pain. So, when meeting potential new suitors we either link so much pain to embarking on a relationship with them that we don't, or our pleasure linked to the feeling of being loved drives us into a new relationship, but then it isn't long before we sabotage the whole thing when our brain remembers what happened last time. Our brain creates stories of pain in our head, which drives us out of that relationship to avoid the imminent pain. And so this vicious cycle continues with our perception of pain in relationships strengthening and being backed up further by each relationship that doesn't last.

I hope now you can see how important it is to question yourself all the time with your thought processes and really spend some time thinking about where your pain-and-pleasure links have come from, and if they are serving you well. For any goal or positive outcome you're going after, if you can master the art of applying pleasure to all stages in the process to get there, then you can change anything and build momentum with it. Both pain and pleasure link directly to every single aspect of our lives – use them, and don't let them use you.

A little exercise for you to do

On the following pages I am going to ask you to think about what you have been procrastinating about and what's freaking you out.

There is space below each part of the exercise so you can write your thoughts. If you run out of space then there is plenty more space at the end of this book. So pick up your pen and start writing...

1. Think about what have you been procrastinating about lately and write down three things that you would love to achieve, whether that's a project that you keep putting off or a diet that you're reluctant to start because birthday celebrations or functions keeping popping up in the calendar; it can be any three things at all.

2. Now write down what is freaking you out about starting to put the work in and achieving each of those three things, and notice the fears that come up. Write down why it's freaking you out and stopping you from doing the work – watch your brain spin out on this because it really does! Keep writing until you're all out of fears.

3. Now take each of those three things and ask yourself what it means for the future if you don't get it done or achieve it. For example, what will happen if you don't ever finish that project for work? What will happen if you allow things in your calendar to keep cropping up stopping you from ever starting your health kick? Think of the compound and ripple effect, and the long-term problems you will face, in relation to finance, health, mood, relationships, etc. Let these ideas spin out for a while and again keep writing them all down until you're all out of consequences.

You should have a pretty meaty list and with it all laid out before your eyes then you should be able to clearly see that you can link far more pain to not getting the three things done which will override the fear you had about doing it at the beginning of the exercise. In fact, it probably makes no sense at all to not get cracking on it right away, as the tasks you've been procrastinating over probably seem like a very small deal now in the grand scheme of things.

Freaking out about things and blowing tiny worries into full-blown fears happens to all of us and we are not to blame as there is a part of our brain that is hardwired to do just that to keep us safe. Coming up next we'll be delving into what is really happening inside of our heads when procrastination sets in.

THE BRAIN

While we've touched on the subject of the brain and its workings, here's a little biology lesson on the three parts of our brain that are responsible for making us feel the way that we do and therefore impact on the action that we take. These are the reptile, mammal and primate brain, also known as the lizard, mouse and monkey – cute, huh?

Although we would assume the monkey brain was the first brain to form, it's actually the last, and it's also the last part of the brain to receive signals from the spinal cord. So unless we get our lizard and mouse in check – feeling understood, safe and part of the group – then we don't get any decent thinking done, and here's why.

The lizard/reptile is the most ancient part of the brain; it's what keeps us alive and is responsible for our survival and maintenance by regulating our heartbeat, breathing and keeping our other vital organs in working order. It is actually hardwired to constantly feel anxious, because its job is to ensure that we are safe and avoiding harm at all times. When our lizard feels safe we feel comfort and peace, but when it's feeling threatened we experience fear.

The mouse/mammal part of the brain regulates our emotions and desires and is particularly responsible for our reward and motivation response. All it wants is for us to feel satisfied and it does this by moving us towards rewards. When the mouse has its needs met we feel content, and when it doesn't we feel frustrated.

The monkey/primate part of the brain handles the higher functions and is really where we do all our best thinking. It regulates feelings and desires, handles complex thinking and reasoning, and forms abstract thoughts while also allowing us to use our imagination and feel empathy. Its main need is connection with others. When the monkey has its needs met, we feel love, and when it doesn't, we experience sorrow and heartache.

Dr Rick Hanson talks of a simplified framework in relation to these parts of the brain, which each concern themselves with safety, satisfaction and connection.[2] Our fundamental needs are:

» To be safe by avoiding harm.

» To be satisfied by approaching reward.

» To be connected by attaching to others.

There are two states: either all three needs are met and our brains default to equilibrium state where the

2. *Dr Rick Hanson, THE BRAIN https://s3.amazonaws.com/nicabm-stealthseminar/Brain2017/NICABM-Brain-Infographic.pdf*

body repairs and refuels itself with feelings of peace, contentment and love, or if one or more of these needs are not met, then the brain fires up in fight-or-flight response, freezes and moves into the reactive mode. During this second state the body's resources are burnt, long-term projects are put on hold, we are destabilised and we feel fear, frustration and heartache.

Cravings, as I'm sure we have all had some experience with, are caused by a deficit in the first and most prehistoric part of the brain. And it's the thoughts and feelings in this first zone that really stand in our way to greatness and GSD-ing (getting shit done.) So, the key to success and growing in life is overcoming and quieting the lizard brain. This requires a certain degree of structural changes to our lives to minimise the lizard brain feeling under attack, but also a large degree of mindfulness is required in the first instance.

Distraction is a great way to stop your lizard brain in its tracks. Distractions come in many forms, some worse than others. You can distract yourself with things like food, alcohol, substances, people, exercise, reading a book or watching a movie. By distracting yourself you will move yourself away from the fear you are feeling, but essentially you are just procrastinating as once the distraction is over you're back at square one again when having to face the same situation or task in hand. Distractions are merely the lizard brain saying, 'here, do this instead, it's safer.'

When you're feeling fear, angst or worry, if you sit there with the feeling long enough you will notice that the fear (or craving) will start small, get stronger... but then it fades away. If you do not act on the impulse to give in or distract, it will eventually pass as the other parts of your brain kick in and start to think rationally.

The problem is that some of us don't sit there with it for as long and immediately soothe the lizard brain by getting ourselves out of that situation and into something else to avoid the potential threat. This part of the brain is like the tiny voice that tells us not to speak up in public, as people may think we're stupid. It tells us not to dress differently, as people will think we're weird. It tells us not to show our vulnerability, as people will take advantage. It tells us that our new creative ideas may not be so great and we should just stick with what we're doing as it's safer. It tells us all these things because staying safe ensures we do not run the risk of being cast out from society, starved and eventually die. It seems pretty daft and rather drastic when you think of it like that, but this part of the brain is prehistoric and only sees things as black and white, one thing or the other. Even entrepreneurs, who have gone so far in breaking through the status quo by combating their lizards and overcoming resistance, still sabotage their efforts at the last minute by allowing their lizard brain to tell them that it's far safer to fail small than to fail big.

Knowledge is power, and when we are aware of how things work it's a lot easier to understand and work with or around them. When you're aware of your lizard brain's workings it's so much easier to recognise its self-sabotaging efforts and get a grip on yourself. Keeping things simple for yourself, and making carefully thought-out decisions each day, will leave you with so much more time on your hands. When you have made a decision that you are going to finish something at the time of starting it, along with the knowledge of how the lizard brain works, you can prepare yourself for the feelings and thoughts that may arise, thus removing the chance of endless procrastination and wasted time with overthinking. It was this type of knowledge that helped me with my mind management to keep me on on track and achieve success with the 7 week bikini show prep that I mentioned earlier.

Here are my top-ten tips for getting your brain working *for* you instead of *against* you:

1. Ask yourself what you feel you are lacking in life, in order to work out if it's a lizard, mouse or monkey problem. Lizard: do you feel anxious and insecure? Mouse: do you lack motivation, gratitude and goals of attainment? Monkey: are you not feeling included, appreciated, liked or loved? Once you have identified where you are lacking, ask yourself how and where you can get more of these experiences.

2. Think back to situations where you felt threatened but it didn't cloud your mind and you were able to handle things easily – what was the difference there?

3. Think back to when you have had good days in the past and your brain felt in a state of equilibrium, then try and repeat these days to reinstall the brain.

4. Make decisions wisely and choose only those that you are 100% committed to.

5. Use 'It' when referring to your lizard brain to separate your emotions.

6. Remain aware of your brain's activity and be mindful of your thought processes.

7. Remember that cultivation undoes craving.

8. Try to ensure you are petting the lizard, feeding the mouse and hugging the monkey, at all times.

9. Remember, pain can be a motivator – use it.

10. And last, I'd like to leave you with this quote from Rick Hanson:

> *I think of the mind as a little bit like a garden. We can practise with it in three fundamentally different ways. We can simply witness the garden, open awareness, bear witness to things, just what's there. I think that's the most fundamental and profound motive engaging the mind in practice. Second, we can pull weeds in the garden; we can reduce the negative or prevent it arising in the first place. That's the second great way to engage the mind. And the third is to grow flowers. It's to cultivate the wholesome. To plant seeds and protect them and fertilise them and so forth until they bear fruit.*[3]

---

3. *Dr Rick Hanson in West Wight Sangha Audio http://west-wight-sangha-audio.blogspot.com/2014/10/pet-lizard-feed-mouse-hug-monkey-by.html*

PART 2

EVEN THE FAKENESS IS FAKE

'Fake it to make it' used to be one of my favourite sayings, and it certainly has helped me in many aspects of work and personal life. Faking certain things has helped to push me outside of my comfort zone, which has forced me to grow. But we can't fake things forever, so it's important to know when the 'make it' part will come so that we can end the façade.

I have faked things like confidence and knowledge until I've become comfortable with them and adopted them as new skills and habits, but there are some things I have tried to fake over the years, e.g. habits and dress styles, which allowed me to fit in with certain peer groups at the time, but have simply left me unsettled, a little at war with myself and questioning my identity after time. And this is a common problem among us today. The rate at which things go viral on the Internet these days, and the speed at which vast amount of trends set in and set off again, so many of us try to keep up with it all and are losing ourselves in the process. In some ways social media has been a wonderful invention in that it allows us to connect with others that are like us, who, due to geographic constraints, we may not have been able to initially connect with in person. But, I also feel that in bringing people together it has also divided them. Now more than ever, people feel the need to join and conform to a certain group's ideals to get on in life. No one wants to be a loner, and we all want to fit in and find others like us, it's human instinct.

But are we joining forces with the right crowd? Are our 'tribes' supporting us, enhancing our natural state and helping us lead happy and balanced lives? Or are they pressurising us, leading us into temptation and enabling us to obsess over our insecurities? It's so tempting to chase the bright shiny things, after all there is an abundance of bright shiny things out there today and as a lot of people are chasing them, it seems we should be too. But for the most part these shiny objects are unobtainable and a lot of us are sacrificing our own happiness in pursuit of them.

People place a huge amount of pressure on themselves to live up to unobtainable standards, which is why we are seeing such a huge increase in mental health issues and such drastic measures being undertaken to obtain the unobtainable.

We live in a world now where breakthroughs are happening all the time. It's wonderful to see things that we thought weren't possible becoming a reality, and when it comes to the self, there is some really impressive work going on with pioneering skin grafts and facial reconstruction, to facial transplants and prosthetic limbs. But there is also the not so positive side.

People were popping out to get boob jobs on their lunch breaks ten years ago, until the lunchtime boob job was banned in 2012, and over the years cosmetic surgery has now become more accessible and more affordable, which has led to the altering of our appearance so drastically and permanently to become completely normalised, which is really quite frightening. Now, I'm not saying that all cosmetic surgery is bad. I have known of many instances when people have undergone breast enlargements, breast reductions and nose jobs for instance and have radically changed into much happier and far more content people who are far more at peace with themselves as a result.

Changing your appearance on the outside can have almost magical powers in transforming you into believing you are someone else, which can give you the confidence to do things that you never thought you could. Transformations that boost confidence and help people to push past their limiting beliefs and prove their own capabilities to themselves, I'm all for. However, not all scars can be seen and sometimes fixing issues on the outside does nothing to help the actual scar on the inside, and the self-image remains poor. The concept of one's self goes much deeper and is more meaningful than the image you see when you look in the mirror, and this is something I feel we need to remind ourselves of.

I caught up with my friend, Laura Kay, who has nearly twenty years' experience in the make-up industry and moved from traditional make-up to permanent make-up in 2013. She is now a leading permanent make-up expert, runs a permanent make-up training academy, and has developed her own line of permanent make-up products. I was interested to hear how she feels the industry has changed over time.

The make-up industry has definitely changed over the years. Before, everyone used to look far more natural and realistic but now, the arena of social media make-up offers a very dramatic, contoured heavy make-up, which is a little bit more theatrical than reality, and we are seeing pictures that are heavily edited and airbrushed. There are a few traditional make-up artists out there who still do the iconic, classic, fresh look, which I love as I'm not a fan of the contoured and heavily made-up look – in reality/daylight it looks a bit strange.

Since the rise of the Kardashians, everyone is trying to seek perfection, hence the rise in cosmetic surgery – everything and everyone is trying to portray a certain look. I'm personally all for plastic surgery if it's going to help you feel better about yourself and boost your self-esteem, but I'm not for people taking it to the extreme where they start to look overfilled and strange.

In my industry, as a permanent make-up artist, I meet and help so many different people helping them to enhance their appearance. I love my job as it incorporates my make-up artist background as well as helping people feel better about themselves and giving them confidence. I've had a few occasions where I have turned people away as I've felt I couldn't manage their expectations and couldn't give them a look that they wanted, e.g. they wanted their eyebrows really thick and I felt it wouldn't suit them, so I would advise them to do more of a subtle enhancement as it's cosmetic tattooing after all and better to start off natural as it's far easier to add than take away!

Laura Kay

Laura isn't the only professional that has had to turn people away. My dear friend Paula Waldman ran her own beauty salon for many years and now has a smaller clientele that she sees privately. She says:

For the last twenty-seven years, I have been working in the aesthetic industry in one form or another. On the surface it can seem like a very superficial profession to be involved in, but actually, the real skill needed to be successful in this profession is to be able to understand human psychology and how emotions, as well as external factors, influence people's desires and decisions.

As a young woman, I remember that a beauty and maintenance regime involved cleanse, tone and moisturise, a visit to the hairdresser every six to eight weeks and maybe a facial once in a while if you were lucky.

As my daughters grew up (they are now twenty-one and twenty-three years old) I stressed the importance of taking care of their nails, hair and skin, providing them with quality skin and hair products. I taught them about looking after the gifts that they had been given. That skin won't stay good if it is mistreated by harsh products, sun tanning and smoking among other things. Without making a big deal about the importance of looking good, it was more to take care of what they already had.

When I first entered the aesthetics industry, most of my clients were ladies between forty and eighty years of age. They were usually quite financially comfortable and just wanted the odd tweak to make themselves look a little better and to hold off, or slow down, the signs of ageing.

As the years have gone on, the clientele has increasingly become younger and younger, and with less disposable income, they push themselves to a financial limit in order to have their aesthetic treatments. This group of clients are not looking for gentle tweaks to slow down the ageing process; they actually want to make physical changes to their faces – bigger lips, higher cheekbones, more defined jawlines.

The responsibility of an aesthetic practitioner is to identify clients with possible body dysmorphia. It is important to ascertain a person's motives for having anti-wrinkle injections or dermal filler injections. Only by doing this can I understand

and manage their expectations. If a person has an unrealistic expectation and seems to be unhappy with numerous aspects of their face and body, they might well be suffering from body dysmorphia. If I suspected this to be the case, I would decline to treat them at that time and refer them to their GP.

But the parameters and guidelines all seem to have gone out of the window, as I would now have to label all twenty- and thirty-somethings as having body dysmorphia. I actually find it sad when a young lady comes to me with the request for treatment that in my opinion is neither indicated or would even look nice. Quite often I will refuse to treat a client under these circumstances. (Unfortunately, not all practitioners are ethical, as is evidenced by a lot of girls and young women that we see today.)

Young people today are not just influenced by magazines to buy the latest skincare or make-up product, they are influenced by what they see on Instagram and other social media sites. There are many reality stars, models and actresses in magazines and on TV that have taken plastic surgery and aesthetic treatments to an extreme. And, because of their popularity, a lot of young people want to try to emulate this.

In reality, these celebrities are enhanced by professional make-up on the red carpet, airbrushed in magazines and use specific apps on their phones that give a perfect photo to put on Instagram. In real life, up close, they would look very different to the 'perfection' that young women are striving to copy. Even the fakeness is fake.

It is these young people who will therefore rarely be happy, or they will find their satisfaction short-lived, and return time and time again to the practitioner still pursuing their ideal of perfection.
Paula Waldman

People hardly think twice about changing their appearance through the use of cosmetic surgery or injectables mainly because everyone else is doing it. They see something they don't like and they find the quickest way to fix it. It doesn't take long to find that solution these days through either word of mouth or via the eye-catching, tempting media displays across the Internet as well as in magazines, newspapers and billboards.

Now, I'm all for being active and making positive changes, but a lot of people nowadays aren't stopping to think carefully about their options and more importantly, explore the issue in depth to find out if there might be something else going on internally that may be clouding their judgement on their external world and their view of themselves.

The problem with not taking the time and going through the appropriate steps to assess where this sudden burning hatred for your nose or your expressive lines is stemming from is that the 'fix' will be very short-lived before the same underlying issue rears its ugly head again, masked in another one of your unique and special features, and then you have to get onto 'fixing' that. It's all one big game of distraction from getting to the root cause and facing the underlying issue.

I believe that every time you alter yourself in such a way, you are reinforcing the idea that you are not good enough and more sadly, you're permanently removing unique parts of you – and once you've started on this self-alteration journey it can be a very slippery slope.

With all these new enticing and quick-fix cosmetic procedures so readily available to us that can instantly lift our mood we have to ask ourselves, do we really all want a piece of it? Is this mood enhancement really going to last as long as the physical? Does altering our appearance this way enhance our lives and make a positive impact, or does it do quite the opposite in the long run? These are really the questions we should be asking ourselves and giving thought to before taking any action, as I don't believe that keeping up with the Kardashians serves many of us well in the long run. So I decided to catch up with a lovely friend of mine, Sarah Moxom, to share with you her own personal journey with cosmetic procedures and aesthetics and to see where it has got her to today both mentally and physically.

> *My journey into cosmetic enhancement and surgery was really one of a broken identity. I truly believe that when people want to passionately and compulsively alter themselves to the extremes of changing facial structures and denying lines and wrinkles, it really comes from a place of pride; broken identity, but also pride. And I think those are really the two underlying reasons that we can see working simultaneously.*

I had an eating disorder when I was sixteen, which critically lasted for two years, but I still had some remnants and remains of the roots of what the eating disorder started from when I came off supervision and was signed off the medical units. I certainly hadn't gone through a long enough journey of healing, physically as well as mentally, before I embarked on a series of cosmetic procedures in my early twenties. I had two boob jobs, a couple of nose jobs, Botox, filler and fat reduction procedures. It was an absolute obsession. I can honestly say that season of my life was one of the darkest and most broken points of my life. There was an unsatisfiable need and desire to change who I was. Nothing was ever enough. There wasn't any amount of cosmetic enhancement that would make me not want to look at something else. It didn't matter what someone told me or didn't tell me.

I found myself surrounded by people who believed that the same thing was right – I was in a culture that set that as a bar when I was young and later encouraged and enforced it, and I accepted those behaviours and patterns and ways of being.

For me it all changed when I met God and I really learnt the truth about where my identity should and does come from.

Ultimately, we are all made beautifully, and there is nothing about any of us that we need to change, it is really the world around us that will endeavour to convince us otherwise. It's trickery, it's lies, it's falsehood and it's not based on any form of truth. I soon realised what I didn't need anymore and that I had allowed vanity, pride and a fractured sense of who I was to take over and to rule my ideas of what beauty was.

So, for me now, it is black and white. No, I will not engage in changing the way I look. I believe that if we are meant to have wrinkles as we get old, then we are meant to have wrinkles. If we are meant to have sagging boobs, then we are meant to have sagging boobs. It is all for good reason and there is nothing that anyone needs to do to change that.

As women we need to stand against ideals and things that have been created to tell us how we should look. I don't ever believe we should follow what the masses are doing.

Sarah Moxom

One in eight adults experience suicidal thoughts and feelings because they are concerned about their body image and according to the ComRes Survery of 2,000 British adults, more than half of eighteen to thirty-four-year-olds feel that reality TV and social media have a negative effect on how they see their bodies.

Social media really preys on your natural human instinct to survive and be approved of, so it's only natural that one might not feel good enough unless one looks a certain way. But it's a loser's game. People can't win – if you have no work done then you'll be criticised for something that doesn't look like an Instagram model, and if you have too much done then you're criticised for having work done.

The big thing here is social acceptance. How do we feel accepted? What makes us feel accepted? Sarah continues:

> *If you are undergoing regular cosmetic surgery and/or aesthetic procedures, do you really know who you are? From my experience, if you don't know who you are when you embark on cosmetic surgery then you don't stop.*

> *It's the culture in the community that we assimilate with that will hugely impact on how we interact and the position that we have with ourselves and among others. How much of what we actually are is made up of who we are internally when we are by ourselves in our alone time (whatever that looks like) and how much of who we are is made up by the people that we identify with? Because my identity wasn't solid, and I didn't feel rooted or grounded, or like I was whole, I would still be massively influenced by the people, or person, who I was with. I suppose we all are to a certain degree.*

> *Anorexia is an addiction and a control mechanism. The root cause of my anorexia was never dealt with at the time – I just looked well enough and no longer like a skeleton, so I was discharged, but then it went into another form because the underlying issues were never dealt with, and so it then just outplayed in a different scenario of cosmetic surgery.*

I was compelled to draw a line on it very recently. Up until a couple of years ago, if I was asked whether I would have cosmetic surgery I would have said 'no', but if asked would I get Botox done every now and again then I would say 'yes, I'm getting a bit older, a few wrinkles here and there, why not?'

This would have been my casual stance, but I started exploring why my exterior was such a big thing for me, and I now truly believe that we should be working on what is in our heart and not how we look with our exterior.

It's now how I make decisions in life and I had to become pretty black and white about it because it was such a toxic part of who I was that I had to make a very clear stand on it. If we don't have positive role models, and we don't speak black and white to younger generations, then it leaves far too much of a grey area that is open to interpretation. If someone looks at me and says, 'she's a really nice person and she's had this done,' then subconsciously they may think: I want to be like her and if she thinks that is OK to do [cosmetic surgery, Botox or fillers] then it's OK for me too. It's too much grey, I don't know how someone is going to interpret that in their lives, and I do feel an element of responsibility for putting people in situations where they may make a decision for themselves based on an unsure sense of identity in themselves, which was triggered by something they have seen on me.

We are leaders in our own lives. We have the ability to impact somebody and that makes us all leaders to anyone looking at us at any given time – it could be someone you just have a conversation with at the gym – you don't know how you impact people every single day. I want people to know their purpose, know who they are, why they are created, love who they are and be driven from the position of their spirit to be better people, not from their physical position.

We are all influencers – within our friendship groups, our work places, etc.

What is the impact that we want to leave? It's not just how you feel about yourself, it's how that is projected onto other people and how that makes them feel.

When you're lying on your deathbed at ninety years old, are you really going to think to yourself: I wish I'd got one more round of Botox?

No, you'll be thinking: what did I do with my life? What kind of impact did I make? What kind of legacy am I leaving behind?

What do you bring to the room? When you walk into a room, what is the impact you want to bring?

I want people to know that they are loved, I want people to know that they are accepted, I want people to feel joy, peace and kindness. That's how I want to be described as and how people see me, not, 'oh, yeah, she's the one with the big boobs,' or, 'she's the one who had a nice outfit.' If that's the only definition that people take away about you, how would that sit with you?

My personal revelation and belief is that I can't control an outcome but I can hopefully plant seeds that will grow themselves in whatever way they do in someone's life. Even if that's just thinking, reflecting, having these conversations or thinking about who we look at on Instagram – whatever that might be – I just believe that wherever we are at with our own journey, healthy conversations will impact us. Healthy communities create healthy change.

Sarah Moxom

DOVE'S STATISTICS

In 2017 the well known personal care brand, Dove, carried out their largest academic report on beauty and confidence. They examined the impact of body esteem, pressures and confidence on girls from all over the globe and found that over half of girls around the world do not have high body esteem. *Over half!*

My heart sank when I read some of the findings in this report although I can't say I was all that surprised.

In over half the girls studied that came in with low body esteem, 7 out of 10 girls were found to have stopped themselves from eating or put their health at risk in some way and 8 out of 10 girls had avoided seeing friends and family or trying out for a team or club due to their lack of self-esteem. With this distinct lack of confidence in themselves and their bodies it's no wonder that it has infiltrated into all areas of their life with 7 out of 10 girls unable to be assertive in their opinion or feel confident enough to stick to their decision.

I was pleased to learn, however, that 7 in 10 girls recognised that there is too much importance placed on beauty as a source of happiness and 8 out of 10 girls said that taking the time to do things that make them feel happy results in making them more confident. This last point is something I truly believe needs to be done in order for us to get more and more comfortable with ourselves and develop our self-assurance and confidence. It's all about finding what makes us tick and doing as much of that as possible to reinforce positive feelings towards ourselves.

I would have hoped for a full house on this next one but unfortunately just under a third of girls interviewed were not aware that images in the media are digitally airbrushed or altered. I feel there's a lot more work to do to create more awareness around this and stop girls creating a warped view of the world and placing unnecessary pressure of unrealistic expectations on themselves and others. It's because of this that I chose to partner with The Girls Network Charity (who you've already supported with the purchase of this book, thank you) and offer myself as a mentor and provide support to their young girls from less advantaged communities.

All the above points touched a nerve with me, as they are all something I truly felt the burden of while growing up. But they are also things I see impacting my friends and clients of all ages today. This is why I feel such a need to address these issues from the inside out as the low self-esteem and a lack in body confidence can have such a rippling and crippling effect on all areas of one's life if not addressed.

PART 3

THE LIPSTICK EFFECT

Lipstick is a bit like war paint; a swipe of lipstick can move me from unenthused to ready to attack the day with enthusiasm in five seconds flat.

According to Wikipedia:

> *The lipstick effect is the theory that when facing an economic crisis consumers will be more willing to buy less costly luxury goods. Instead of buying expensive fur coats, for example, people will buy expensive lipstick. The underlying assumption is that consumers will buy luxury goods even if there is a crisis. When consumer's trust in the economy is dwindling, consumers will buy goods that have less impact on their available funds. Outside the cosmetics market, consumers could be tempted to by expensive beer or smaller, less costly gadgets.[4]*

---

4. https://en.wikipedia.org/wiki/Lipstick_effect

It makes a lot of sense when you think about it. Cosmetics are not just functional items, they are also luxury goods. In our little history lesson at the beginning of this book we noted that lipsticks were the most popular purchase back in the 1920s and 1930s as they were colourful and cheap. Well, the same applies today with their price point in relation to the other cosmetic purchases one could make, so it's no wonder we find ourselves at the make-up counter to make us feel better on a crap day.

Cosmetics in their pretty packaging have become somewhat of a status symbol. Just as Apple and its iPhones, Chanel and its lipsticks work the same way in validating ourselves.

I'm a firm believer that you should do whatever it takes to make yourself feel better, so if that's paying over the odds for a swanky new lipstick then so be it!

Like most, I too am a sucker for pretty packaging, and while I do not overly concern myself with designer labels usually, you'll still find me at the sunglasses counter at the airport paying way over the odds for a pair of designer sunglasses before jetting off on holiday. It's almost as if money doesn't count in the airport?! But I am human, I have my moments of weakness and I too am capable of throwing all rationalisation out of the window and shopping on impulse. In today's world personal power is equivalent to purchasing power and it's not just a marketing ploy, it's actually a psychological condition.

The more expensive something is the more exclusive and desirable it becomes, which is why high-end brands do not throw low-priced items in with their collections. Luxury brands are particularly reluctant to offer markdowns, as they fear it will dilute the power of the brand and its exclusivity. Higher-end brands tend to produce their products in Europe, which is significantly more costly to do than in Asia, and let's not dismiss the 'limited edition' pieces that are produced in even smaller runs, which ramps up costs in comparison to producing them in bulk.

In my opinion, high-end fashion brands also like to waste time. The research and talent that is involved behind the scenes is extremely costly to the end user. High-end brands spend a lot of time and effort creating only one piece, which is arguably quite unnecessary – they overcomplicate things for the sake of it and we end up paying dearly for it.

Fashion shoots are particularly expensive to organise, not to mention the cost of placing the final images on billboards or in magazines. So when you're paying higher-end prices for these luxury items, remember that you're mainly paying for the brand's choice of production, the pay cheques of the many people behind it and the advert that showed it to you. Furthermore, high-end, luxury fashion brands raise their prices for literally no reason other than to increase their appeal at the upper end so that they attract new and wealthier customers.

So, back to cosmetics and the luxury brand versions; are you really getting a better product than if you were to purchase similar from the high street at a fraction of the cost?

Fragrance, which is one area that designer brands spend a bit more time on – a nice fragrance doesn't make the product function any better but you're still paying for it. On the flip side, some brands may state their products as 'fragrance free' and still overcharge as we automatically believe it's better for our skin and hypoallergenic, which you'll be learning in the next chapter is total BS.

Then there are the applicators that come with most designer make-up. These are generally thrown away because we've spent our money on the expensive designer brushes and beauty blenders, so you've paid for that which you have no use for.

But the ingredients must be of better quality, surely? Sadly no, the ingredients are mainly the same as your high street brands – some of the products even come out of the same factory.

And not forgetting the pièce de résistance – that pretty packaging. Oh, yes, you're paying for that box that you immediately throw out, the tub or tube that is discarded after use, and all the designers' salaries that went into making them. Luxury packaging not only validates the product, but it also validates us as the purchaser too. As most people are amateurs when it comes to buying make-up, we subconsciously believe that if the packaging is pretty, then the product inside will make us pretty too. Our purchase choices are made on an emotional level and when it comes to beauty, it's all about the romance, right?

Remember, you are mainly paying for a brand name, which is a status symbol. If that is hugely important to you then crack on, I won't judge, but if you'd rather move past that and save yourself a few quid then do your best to think rationally when shopping for cosmetics and ignore the outer shell; bargains can be just as powerful and also rather personally liberating, you know.

BAD BEAUTY INDUSTRY

As I sit here flicking through a beauty industry magazine I feel a sudden sense of overwhelm and exhaustion set in.

I'm already a month late getting round to reading this and with my day having started at 4.30 a.m. I'm tired and a little cranky as it is, but while I study all the new and innovative products and technology that are pasted across the pages before me I can't help thinking: does the world really need all of this?

Featured in just the few pages I've got through so far are multiple new laser hair removal machines, new LED skin rejuvenation and micro-current facial toning technology, multiple machines for non-surgical face and body treatments followed by even more state-of-the-art laser machines offering laser body sculpting and further non-invasive facial and body contouring platforms.

Interspersed with all this new technology I have also learnt that Bio Sculpture seem to be making a comeback with their ethos range; another company has created a DIY equivalent to a chemical peel, promising easy application and immediate results in just two steps, and there is now a new youth supplement on the market that has linked the relationship between the gut and the skin, which is apparently 'packaged for optimum results!'

I have been served up facts and figures: 83% of beauty therapists have had to correct another therapist's bad work, CBD oil, peptides and probiotics are apparently the new trending skincare ingredients. Oh, and pretty corals, ice-cream inspired pastels, neon brights and barely there nudes are supposedly all on-trend for this summer. Excuse my French, but that's a lot of new shit going on! Where the hell does one even start?

And this is exactly the type of mental exhaustion I've been feeling towards my industry for sometime now. I'm all for breakthrough technology, helping people feel better about themselves by addressing personal issues, solving problems or just brightening up their day with pretty nail polish; however, the rate at which all this innovative technology and 'miracle' products are being churned out leaves me feeling rather suspicious of their makers' claims, which are written in bold statements across the advertorials, depicted in the happy and smiley faces staring out from the pages before me, or demonstrated in rather astounding before and after photos.

I try to live optimistically, but when it comes to my industry and the claims that are made, I far too often smell a rat. And I'm sure we're all aware of the old adage, 'if it sounds too good to be true, then it probably is.'

So I began conducting a little research into these cosmetic brands, their products and their claims, and during my investigation I stumbled across a lady named Rowena Bernado.

A former marketing manager turned beauty bullshit buster, Rowena Bernado no longer works for 'them' and works for 'us' in stripping the wool from our eyes. She writes a blog called 'Beauty and the Bullshit' and I wondered if she would perhaps be willing to speak to me and give me some nuggets of wisdom to help me paint the not-so-pretty picture for you all.

After tracking her down on Instagram, and reaching out to her about this little book I'm writing, I was thrilled to hear her support in my quest to expose the beauty brands' unsavoury marketing techniques. After a few DMs back and forth, we eventually hopped on a Face Time call for a good old chinwag about all things beauty, some things life, and all the bullshit.

Rowena is like the tough, loving, fairy godmother of this chapter, who has come to rip off those rose-tinted spectacles, toss them to the floor and stamp around on them for good measure.

Her life has been fascinating and I was gripped listening to all the exciting things she has been up to and the self-discoveries she has made on her life journey so far. Her career has taken many twists and turns, and she's certainly had some adventure over the years.

After graduating in mechanical engineering, she was reviewing for the board exam when a blind job advert caught her eye, which turned out to be a marketing role at Unilever.

Out of 20,000 applicants that applied, Rowena and just one other were taken on, so she switched her engineering plans to delve into the world of beauty marketing.

She comes from a family of inventors, and I was pleased to learn that the inventing genes have not skipped a generation, as she currently has two patents to her name. Both are fashion-related utility models – one is a bag that becomes 13 bags, and the other is a style accessory that prevents you from losing your glasses – both things that could come in handy for a lot of us I'm sure.

Though she is fully trained in marketing, and obviously knows her stuff, she said: *'I just didn't want to do it anymore, I just do not believe in how it has evolved void of respect of its consumers, it's "milking cows".'*

For her own inventions, she decided to partner up with somebody else to do the manufacturing, marketing, distribution and management. A very smart move, as I know from my own experience that mastering the art of marketing has the tendency to rip all the fun and excitement right out of the thing that was so lovingly created.

I asked her if she felt that marketing today was different from how it used to be, to which she responded:

> *It's becoming more vicious, I think, it just doesn't respect your space anymore. The medium has changed as before we just had TV and merchandising, now it invades you in your phones, in your daily life, and although I could adapt to it, I am pissed off when I see an advertisement on my phone, so I don't want to do something that I, myself, don't want to be subjected to.*

Rowena is going to share with us some serious juicy facts on what I like to call the 'Beauty Bullshit Buster' section of the book. But before we get onto all of that I want to share with you some pearls of wisdom I picked up from my call with her.

We start with a trip back to her beauty marketing days; she tells me a lot has happened in between, but it all starts in her home country in Asia.

When the Asian crisis happened, beauty companies she was consulting to had left their ambitions to expand distribution in Asia, so she decided to pack her bags and set off for Paris. She stopped in Dubai beforehand where she worked for a little while to earn enough money to set herself up and pay her first year's rent, and then she eventually moved on to Paris with bags of enthusiasm and started sending out her CVs.

She sent out about 74 CVs, but the Parisians weren't particularly welcoming to her as a foreigner, and she barely got any response at all. She then found herself in a very unfortunate situation where her life savings were spent by someone she trusted and the need for a job, any job, was desperate. She started waitressing and even considered a job as Euro Disney's Pocahontas (albeit foiled by a visa technicality).

It was a very tough time, but eventually she figured it out and she did this by enlisting the help of the French arm of the international organisation called Mensa that she is a member of. She approached them and told them about her idea and they backed her with some investment for her project. With their support Rowena started her consulting business, and with her knowledge of the

Asian market and varied cosmetic brands, she began consulting to cosmetic companies in Europe – instead of them hiring an Asian, they hired a French consulting company, and that's how she got her foot in the global door.

> *It was difficult, I really started from the trenches; no money, no house, no family and barely speaking the language – but you figure things out until... voilà!*

Rowena worked her way into the hub and centre of beauty marketing where she got to decide which products went forward, what their image would be, what the shades would be called, etc. Naming shades seems to be Rowena's favourite part of the job – I mean, who wouldn't want to think up cool, sexy and emotive product names for a living, eh?

She handled a lot of brands on a distribution and creation level, the last being the Top 18 Global Make-up Brands. She researched what was happening with other brands and their competitors, and got to know all the suppliers, and it's from all of this that she is able to provide us with such juicy inside knowledge coming up in the next few pages.

It wasn't long, however, that working in the heart of the beauty industry got tiresome and Rowena felt that she really wasn't learning anything. So, despite a good income, she felt it was time for a change and to move on to something that would serve her better. After almost twenty-five years of working in all the axes of the beauty industry, a fire of fury sparked within her and led her to start her blog, 'Beauty and the Bullshit', as soon as she left.

Prior to biting the bullet and leaving she had thought many times that she didn't want to work in cosmetics anymore, but it was a tough decision to make, and a very difficult one to come to terms with as she was hating something that was essentially putting food on her table. She told me:

> *To do a good job I have to make women feel terrible about themselves. My objective is I want 10% growth next year. That means you, who are spending £100, will have to spend £110 next year; it doesn't matter if you have all the make-up in the world, I will make you want more. I could do that quite fabulously but my soul is burning in hell. It wasn't good. I was selling enough lipsticks to fill 30 Olympic-sized swimming pools. So, can you imagine that much waste as well in terms of plastic?*

Rowena really struggled with this because as much as she hated it, that was exactly what she was trained to do, and she worried about what else she could do if she left and what else she could do to get her income.

> *I was at a loss for a while, but now I've found my centre. I said, 'well, I'll solve it from the root, I'm not going to hate cosmetics but I have to make sure that women buy it for the right reasons. You don't need a 65th version of Viva Glam. Find a shade of red and stick to it.'*

This was the motivation for her blog.

> *We don't feel good about ourselves anymore. We're listening to everyone and not listening to*

what is inside of us. What we consider beautiful is that which makes us look rich. In Europe you will have a fake tan, or you will tan yourself and risk getting cancer just so that you look like you can afford a vacation every weekend. That's not healthy.

People in Asia are bleaching themselves. That's not healthy — it's so unhealthy, and all because of what is considered beautiful is somebody who looks rich. Then we so value youth that when we start ageing, we inject ourselves with so many things. We refuse to grow old; we refuse to acknowledge the beauty in wisdom and old age. That's not right. The more we taunt old age, the more we are afraid of it and the more we consume to hold on to the inevitable change.

I'm embracing my old age. I've been doing the bullshitting so I don't fall into the trap of my own bullshit, but what about the women that I'm saying have to look white, have to look bronzed? It's not healthy. So forget about looking rich, looking young, you have to embrace your own constitution. If you are born with hips, embrace them. If you are born thin, embrace it. There is no such thing as beauty trends; beauty trends are bullshit. They are only created to make us buy more.

Solve it from the root. Embrace your own beauty. Don't envy other women. Your beauty is yours. I have mine. Not because you are beautiful do I become less beautiful. We are different and *that's what is beautiful about it. If we all looked the same, how would we know beauty?*

Let's take back the definition of beauty. We do not let the beauty industry, who has vested interest in our self-doubt, tell us that we are beautiful; we tell ourselves that we are beautiful, we embrace ourselves – whatever age, whatever colour, however we look.

But be healthy, I draw the line there.

You don't swim in potato chips and then display yourself twerking, and when people critique you, you say you're being bullied, that's not the way to do it either. Be healthy, listen to your body – what is healthy with you? Trust in the inner voice and listen to it. Now we are so flooded with all these ads that we don't know what is true anymore, but what is true is inside of us. Then there is this competition among ourselves – we shouldn't be competing, we are sisters but we are made to feel that every girl is a competition. It's not healthy.

If we feel good about ourselves then we consume less, and if we consume less then it is much better for nature. At the end of the day what is really good for us is also good for the planet, but we have to discern from inside of ourselves what is really good for us. It is not an industry that profits from us telling ourselves this, so we need to do the work and trust our inner voice.

I asked Rowena if she felt that working in that environment within the beauty industry had changed her views of herself, made her insecure, or made her see parts of her body in a negative way to which she responded:

> *No, not at all because I knew what I was saying was bullshit. My other co-workers, however, believed in their own bullshit and that was very risky. I was one of those that never believed what I was saying. The top management is all men. They just want the bottom line; they just want more and more sales. They didn't care how we got to them, so long as the bottom line was OK, they were OK. It's the women who are designing everything (because we would know!) all the other girls unfortunately believed their own BS. I always knew what I was doing was bullshit and I don't want that on my epitaph – 'Here is Rowena, she sold so many lipsticks' – no, that is not how I want it. My life is worth more than selling lipsticks. I want to be kind.*

I asked Rowena what is next for her and her response really did make me chuckle – the gal's got a point here:

> *I have a blog coming up called 'Science You Bitch' because science is everybody's bitch! We trash everything in the name of science. A scientist is somebody who is not afraid to be proven wrong, and an artist is somebody who is not afraid to have their heart broken.*

So now on to the nitty-gritty and the part of the book I was perhaps the most excited to share with you. Coming up, and fresh off the 'Beauty and the Bullshit' blog, you'll find Rowena's 'Ten Worst Reasons to Buy Cosmetics' and the five tricks Rowena used to make you spend your money.

Rowena's 'Ten Worst Reasons to Buy Cosmetics'[5]

1. Because it is expensive.

A product is expensive because it chooses to be so. It has a higher profit margin because it has to pay for seals of approval, advertising, endorsers and its exclusive distribution channel. A higher percentage of the product cost goes to packaging, not the formula. Expensive is not an assurance that a product is good. Most times you can find exact replicas of expensive products in a mass-market brand in less flashy packaging. (However, if you are buying expensive so you can brag to your friends, that is another issue altogether.)

2. Because X% of women agree that...

Ah, lying with statistics! All it takes to get a favourable statistical result is a well-chosen panel size and ambiguous questions. And if that test can be done in-house, which it almost always is, even better. And besides, your beauty is unique. No matter if 100% of women agree, they are not you, are they?

---

5. *http://beautyandthebullshit.blogspot.com*

3. Because it is hypoallergenic.

If you are not particularly allergic to a certain ingredient, why go for a hypoallergenic brand that rids itself of fragrances so that all active ingredients then pay dearly for it? It is a manic preoccupation with needless sanitation that is costing you dearly. And get this: the term hypoallergenic is 'self-controlled' – FDA/EC has no predefined/accepted definition for it.

4. Because it is natural.

Forgoing the obvious argument that everything surrounding us comes from nature and is thus natural, there is no one guideline or regulation about where to draw the line and what can be claimed natural.

Though I acknowledge every woman's desire for natural cosmetics even as we regularly stuff our faces with bacon and alcohol – natural is simply logistically undeliverable without a dose of BS and self-denial.

5. Because it has patented innovation.

This is how it works: if you tweak the percentage of an ingredient in a formula, or change three dimensions of your packaging, you can already file for a patent. That doesn't mean it will be approved though – the process can take months to years, and most times the patent will be disapproved or just dropped. But the beauty is that the company can claim to have a patent pending innovation, and rake in sales.

Patented? Just say no.

6. Because it is kind to animals.

All products are subject to the same rules and are in the same boat. They all use ingredients that have been previously tested on animals, otherwise, they would not get approval to trade.

But the good news for animal lovers is that companies are not required to do additional testing for ingredients that have been previously tested nor are they allowed to test some more for cosmetic purposes.

7. Because it is dermatologically tested.

A corollary of the medical practitioner's seal of approval.

Of all the claims a product can have, this is the most meaningless. Just ask this question: dermatologically tested for what?

8. Because it has a (pseudo-) medical practitioner's seal of approval.

Here's the deal: all commercially marketed products have to comply with one regulating body that sets the rules of what is safe for consumption. That regulating body (can be FDA/ EC/JP – depending on the country) has standard regulations, procedures and government-set fees.

When a seal of approval is given by other medical and pseudo-medical associations, it does not mean that a product complied with additional standards. It means that the brand outbid other brands to pay a large sum to get the exclusive seal of approval. This large amount goes into the association's coffers, controlled by the association's officers.

9. Because it contains the ingredient proven/known to cure...

Whenever you see this claim and feel swayed by it, walk away. It is a common play on words used by marketers to mislead. The product contains the ingredient but in proportions too small to deliver the benefit, yet enough to get away with claiming that the ingredient is there.

10. Because some proceeds go to charity.

Cosmetic companies identify with charities that they know their customers will like (children, animals, nature, aids, women-related issues) and they donate a minuscule amount to the charity's high visibility PR programmes and write off their expenses against taxes.

Want to *really* help charity? Skip the mediocre lip gloss, let the cosmetic company pay their due in taxes that help propel the nation's growth and donate straight to the charity of your choice without commercial intermediaries.

Top 5 Tricks Rowena uses to make you spend money

1. ## Sex up the shade name.

   Take Nars' Orgasm Lip Gloss for example, whether to say you are disappointed by the orgasm, you are buying an orgasm, you would like a second orgasm, you have run out of orgasm – it is a great story! Do not just give me a cheek blush, give me a good story – give me a conversation piece, make me feel naughty, reckless, alive, heck, liven up my life – give me orgasm.

2. ## Pimp the claim.

   Consider this real story:

   Old:

   Rich Colour Lipstick. Creamy colour that shapes and defines lips. Wider coverage for easier application. Non-feathering. SPF 15 with Vitamins A and E.

   New:

   Vivid lipstick. With 3D pigments for vivid lips and vivid life! Marigold extract has moisturising properties for 96%* more sensuous lips. SPF 15.

   *Bullshit research, details of which you do not need to see conducted on 26 women or so.

   What is the difference between the old and the new?

   Nothing: *nada, zilch, niente.*

But of course, I will tweak the line up a little so it will not be too obvious to you. This is how I will further cloud your perception. I will also:

- discontinue some worse selling shades (which are bound to be someone's favourite shade – but I don't care)

- put in some wilder colours to give you the impression that our line-up is exciting. They most probably won't sell as individual shades, but it will lift the sales of the whole line. Unquantifiable but true

- sex up the shade names (tactic N°1)

- I will throw in some research where I will be claiming high percentage of women who noticed a more moisturised lip

- price the lipstick just a tad higher for credibility.

And the result:

Long-term consumers liked the 'new' vivid lipstick better and swore that it had better properties than the old one. Sales were up by 35%. True story.

You see, of course, we are all prone to the power of suggestion. If we are hyped that something is better, we will believe and perceive that it is.

Such is how we operate in the biz.

3. Shoot statistics with steroids.

Give me any crappy product and I can weave a convincing steroid-shot statistic about it. How? Just a good-sized panel and lots of ambiguity.

First I choose a big enough panel (a group of testers) so that even if I get one or two negative answers, the percentage of positives is still a high enough number.

To illustrate:

- In a panel of 6, if 2 said no – that means 4/6 or 67% positive feedback. Not good

- In a panel of 10, if 2 said no – that means 8/10 or 80% positive feedback. Good but not high enough

- In a panel of 20, if 2 said no – that means 18/20 or 90% positive feedback. That is good!

So, my panel size has to be at least 20. Can be much more but that unnecessarily increases my costs.

Then, I ask my panel an ambiguous question where a positive answer is almost inevitable.

For example:

Test 1:

Lab Tech: Did you notice a difference in moisture of your lips when you applied the lipstick?

Tester: Well... just very slightly.

Lab Tech: So, that's a yes. Thank you.

Test 2:

Lab Tech: Did you notice a difference in moisture of your lips when you applied the lipstick?

Tester: Yes. It felt drier.

Lab tech: Yes or no only please. Did you notice a difference?

Tester: *Yes – but...*

Lab Tech: That will be all, thank you.

Lab tech writes:

I therefore conclude that out of 23 women tested, 100% found a difference in their moisture level after lipstick application.

4. **If you can't blind them with brilliance, baffle them with bullshit – Ancient marketing adage.**

   Fame = Value. Fact.

   i) Celebrities, actresses, models, singers, TV personalities, athletes – are our obvious partners, but those who 'touch' celebrities also have the ability to reflect celebrity mind-blinding brilliance – think make-up artists, hairdressers and stylists.

   Medical professionals also partake in the endorsement game.

- Dentists endorsing a brand of toothbrush/ toothpaste/mouthwash. (OK, so dentists are quasi-doctors, but you get my drift.)

- Dental associations giving their seal of approval to the highest bidder. (This is *soooo* corrupt and big money goes to association officers.)

- 'Celebrity' dermatologists acting as spokespersons for any brand

- Any professional acting as spokesperson for a company's germ or disease scare tactic.

Consumers pay these so-called professionals for an unbiased opinion!

ii) 'Unbiased Journalists'

Journalists can be so damn dirty with product endorsements! Magazine covers are for sale for the companies' celebrity endorsers, or whole segments of documentaries are produced on contamination and then followed by a soap commercial. Even supposed neutral documentaries are actually testimonials on products – skin care and slimming information integrated in content with purchase of commercials.

You say that these goodie bags, fees, gifts, fancy event invitations, do not affect a writer's opinion? Whatever.

Beauty brands can 'buy' an award from the magazine editor! (Which they stick shamelessly at the shelves next to their products.)

5.   Patents and trademarks

Trademarks – give it a snazzy logo, and a 'scientific' illustration of silver hexagons and double helixes, and trademark the damn thing.

What can you patent really?

You cannot patent just anything, silly! You must have something über-extraordinary such as:

* A 'miracle' formula. If you use whale sperm extract like everybody else, why, you can still patent your formula to contain 1.2875% whale sperm, while the rest of the world use 1.28748%. And don't be shy about it – miracle worker you

* A 'magic' ingredient. What? Your sperm extract comes only from Atlantic-swimming albino whales? Extra patent points for you, oh pioneering one

* An 'innovative' container. Increase the diameter of your competitor's lipstick case by 0.025mm, change its curve by 0.0025° and round the edges 0.0018mm more and voilà! Don't see a difference? Well, numbers don't lie – so advance to *GO* and collect £200. Your 'innovative' case is now patent worthy

- A 'special' delivery system. So, you think my mascara wand looks like any other? Well, mine has exactly 207 hair filaments, which are 3 cm long twisted 8.5 times with a torque of 500 joules in a 0.02 mm wire*. Who is special now? *I might not be making sense here, forgot most of my engineering studies you see

- A 'pioneering' idea. Hmm, seems to me that none of my competitors has thought of patenting this idea we all are using. Well let me do it for them then and sue the ass off everybody else!

Pending Patent – disapproved or not, it doesn't really matter.

I can already advertise that I have a patent pending application and give you all the illusion that I have the fountain of youth in my hands. What's important is that I was able to launch with a big bang, made a mark on you dear consumers with an illusion of a miracle, who in turn gave the Council of the Clueless enough money to wipe their arses with.

THE MEDIA AND DIGITAL OVERLOAD

These days we are more distracted than ever and our attention spans have plummeted. We use multiple devices and screens at high rates, and often at the same time. Have you ever found yourself searching for something on your phone while watching TV and also working on your laptop at the same time?

Our attention spans are now just an average of eight seconds (advertisers probably have a better chance of keeping a goldfish's attention than the average person) so you can understand what marketers are up against and why they've had to get smart about their ways.

Our mobile device use is at an all-time high and our attention spans are at an all-time low, so marketers are shifting their focus in order to break through the 'digital noise' and be heard. The online world has become so saturated by digital ads, and while we believe we are being smart by ignoring or actively avoiding them, I'm afraid the machines are always one step ahead.

In today's world everyone has a smartphone, and most of us have multiple smart devices in the form of tablets, phones and computers. If you couple this with the rise of data, digital marketing tools and social media, marketers actually have a wealth of knowledge and power to pinpoint us with advertising messages.

Brands know that if they stand for something, rather than just selling something, they will boost loyalty and win buy-in from potential customers. Predictive analytics use big data technology and machine learning to identify those of us with a high propensity to purchase, which enables marketers to target you at the right time and turn you from a browser into a buyer. Artificial intelligence and machine learning is being used to analyse billions of clicks and differentiate between a browser and a buyer, before you've even made your intentions known.

By monitoring all your previous interactions, AI technologies are able to identify highly specific, individualised aesthetics and then tailor everything from colours, copy, images and other elements to ensure that you respond well and increase your chances of purchase.

Brands are now focussing on the individual customer journey, which can be complex but also surprisingly predictable. They can anticipate your behaviour and then automate the best response to you from identifying a whole host of variables from which device you're on, time of day, local weather, recent purchases, etc. Clever stuff, eh? And all just a little bit scary.

SOCIAL MEDIA

Did you know that social media can be as habit-forming as cocaine? The more you use it, the more addictive it gets, and there are plenty of studies out there to confirm this.

The average person spends more than five years of their life on social networks, so it's no wonder this digital habit of ours can be as hard as giving up smoking.

When used right, social media can be a wonderful tool to add value to our lives – it can connect us with people, help us grow relationships and bring new discoveries to our attention. But it also has a very dark side by negatively impacting our productivity and encouraging us to constantly compare our lives to those of others, which is hugely detrimental to our mental health.

We need to understand that we are being played here.

Social networks are designed to get us hooked, so it's not our fault for wasting hours of our time on these platforms that have been so cleverly created to make us repeatedly use them. If you think it's just you, look at the sheer volume of social media blocking apps available to download – I can assure you, you are not alone and it is very much something that a lot of us are struggling to get a grip on.

Unfortunately, there is no filter when it comes to viewing social media. On a subconscious level we absorb far more than our brains can cope with, as we didn't actively seek or search for the information, it was just fed to us. It's called a 'feed' for a reason, you know.

Our mindset plays an important part in how we view and absorb information. If we're not in the right frame of mind when data is fed to us, then on a subconscious level it can actually have serious implications on our entire outlook, and with this happening again and again over time it's extremely easy to get stuck in a rut.

I have some days when I relish everyone's posts – I pass comment and react to statuses, scrolling through in a happy daze. I will smile, laugh out loud, feel tears prickling at the happy or sad news, and feel confident in my position to show emotion at others' posts. But there are other days when I'm not feeling as strong and as altogether. And I can tell you that these days are often more frequent.

I'll still scroll along but with a negative mindset. Those happy posts from others I still feel happy for, but it's muted because the further I scroll, the more the sense of underachievement and inadequacy takes hold on me. My mind can be my worst enemy; I'm sure yours can be too, but don't worry, we'll be getting on to seeing to that shortly.

Unfortunately, like an addiction, once you board the lousy mindset wagon, it can be very hard to get off. Social media feeds are with us all day long – in our hands, pockets or handbags – a depression-fix is really just one tap away.

So, how do we stop getting sucked into the vortex of negative and deprecating self-talk that social media can prompt within ourselves?

Awareness and acceptance of what's really going on here is a start, but unfortunately there is no simple fix. Specific platforms may die out, but new ones will emerge in their place; social media is here to stay, so we're just going to have to deal with it.

To simply remove yourself from social media altogether suits some – I know a few that have done it and have been living much calmer and balanced lives since doing so, but I also know others who have tried and failed.

For most of us, removing ourselves completely, only temporarily fixes the issue; the dreaded FOMO (fear of missing out) tends to always lead us back. For many, social media is a big part of working life whether you run your own business or the company that you work for requires you to have an online presence.

Increasing our awareness within ourselves, being mindful and putting some tools in place to help overcome the negative responses within our mind, is really the only solution.

Five Tips for Pulling out of the Social Media Vortex

1. Get your shoes on and walk out the door – look at the sky, look at the trees, notice the cracks in the pavement, there's an actual physical world out there, people!

2. Turn off notifications on your phone. All of them! I can't tell you how much my anxiety levels have dropped since turning all Facebook, Instagram, Messenger and WhatsApp notifications completely off!

3. Better still, remove social media apps from your phone so that you have to physically go to another source such as a computer or laptop to access them. I tried this and failed, I hope you will succeed.

4. Allocate time slots in the day that you are allowed to check social media and stick to them. For me, this one is a hard one to master as the frequency and length of time slots increases over time, and before I know it the whole system has gone out the window.

5. Have an entire day off (or maybe two) and really notice how you feel and the difference it makes to your productivity, mood and state of mind. Try this experiment repeatedly

(and for longer periods if possible) to break the habit. Question your relationship and re-form your association with social media. I did this, it works, it's how I came to the compromise of switching off all notifications, which I will say again has added a lot more peace and calm to my days.

PART 4

WHAT GOES IN MUST COME OUT

It is impossible to stop the signs of ageing happening altogether. Fact.

Just like you can't run off a bad diet for a weight loss goal, you can't cream over a bad diet to reduce the ageing process either.

What you put in is what you get out.

I'm sorry to burst your bubble but there are no miracle creams out there that can singlehandedly reverse the signs of ageing or fix your skin woes in one or even five hundred applications.

Since they are not classified as drugs, the FDA law does not require cosmetic products to have FDA approval before they go on the market. So, no matter how expensive the price tag or how many exotic ingredients it may seem to contain, any skincare product that doesn't need a doctor's prescription is not required to undergo scientific research to prove its effectiveness.

Now, this isn't to say that certain products won't help improve your appearance. Some skincare products are smart and can provide additional moisture or help blur over your wrinkles with a high silicone content. However, skincare products are only meant to support good lifestyle habits to keep your skin healthy and looking youthful, so anything claiming to do more than that is simply lies.

Beauty comes from within, in more ways than one – if you want to visibly improve what's on the outside you'll have to start changing what's going on in the inside.

I'm going to keep things pretty simple here, because everything your body needs to function at its best can be found in the basic foods available to us at the supermarket and grocery store, and also a lot of it is common sense.

We have a tendency to overcomplicate things and we make everything so much harder for ourselves when we do. It's not necessary to spend your hard-earned money on dietary supplements, or waste time researching and purchasing the latest super food. Supplements, and some less common foods may have some advantages, but until you get the basics right none of that stuff is going to matter anyway.

We only require basic things to keep our bodies and organs at optimal nutritional health. It's a simple of case of eating the right amount of the good stuff, which is readily available to us, and most of it does not come in pretty packaging.

I said there is no magic cream, but there is one particular lotion that you can use on your skin to prevent damage before it starts, and that is sunscreen – use it every day without fail. Incorporate it into your daily routine or ensure that your foundation, BB cream, tinted moisturiser (or whatever) has a high SPF of at least 35 that protects against both UVA and UVB rays.

The visible ageing process on our skin is simple to understand. As we age our bodies produce less collagen, which is the main structural protein that keeps our skin supple. With less collagen being produced as we grow older (an inevitable part of the natural ageing process) wrinkles will appear. Under the microscope, a biopsy of a wrinkle shows no signs that it's actually a wrinkle. Wrinkles are simply your skin's way of relaxing; there is no shame in that. They are part of you and really shouldn't have any negativity associated with them at all.

You can do all the right things but you can't argue with nature and its natural processes, so stop wearing yourself out and crippling yourself financially trying. Why not instead turn your focus to the things that you do have control over? And address the things that will have a far bigger impact on your overall well-being than hiding a few wrinkles, like how you're fuelling your body for performance mentally and physically for instance.

Before we move on, I'd just like to recap. When skincare products are used in conjunction with a healthy lifestyle, it is entirely possible to improve the visible effects of ageing on the skin, but it's impossible to stop it from happening altogether.

Unless the lotions, creams, sprays, and ointments you're putting on your skin have been prescribed by a doctor, then they have not undergone any type of scientific research, much less a study that proves their effectiveness in reducing wrinkles or boosting skin health.

My dear friend, Andrea Dann, is a physique and diet-management coach, who I've been friends with for nearly ten years now, and she has become more like a sister to me in recent years. She has completely transformed my relationship with food and exercise, which in turn has transformed my entire life. Through experimentation with myself, guided by Andrea's advice, I have learnt so much about the way my body reacts to what I put into it in relation to what I get out of it.

Andrea has had amazing results with her clients; she has prepped herself for many bodybuilding shows and coached me for my bikini show last year. She is passionate about the way our bodies work, and she's a complete fountain of knowledge when it comes to the way the things we eat impacts us. She loves the science of how our bodies process foods and she is constantly studying it within her clients as well as within herself to see how different foods affect different people. With a lot of her time each day spent in the gym you may be surprised to know that what goes on in the kitchen is actually far more important than what goes on in the gym when it comes to physique.

So, there was no way I wasn't going to share some of Andrea's top tips and pearls of wisdom with you which have had such a powerful effect on my own emotional and physical well-being. Over in the next chapter, Andrea and I have put together some rather simple and super important facts that can improve your well-being no end, and increase your chances of diet success and better health all round.

SLEEP, EAT, TRAIN, REPEAT

The more focus you place on each of these three, the better the effect will be on your hormones, which is what your body is run by and will affect all areas of your life physically and mentally. You *are* hormones. Your whole body is conducted by hormones. Everything you are, everything you think about, how much body weight you hold, how well you sleep, how well you digest your food – everything.

SLEEP

Sleep is number one. Sleep loss limits fat loss. Lack of sleep increases insulin resistance, which increases your fat gain. Lack of sleep increases cortisol, which slows down your metabolism and decreases your thyroid function. And sleep loss also increases blood pressure.

More sleep and less training is recommended for people trying to get fit, and for athletes. Overtraining and over-cardio is actually raising cortisol, raising stress and raising anxiety, which in turn makes people unable to sleep.

We are run by a natural and internal process that regulates our sleep-wake cycle each twenty-four hours. If there is light coming through your curtains, or a laptop on in the corner, your body thinks it's daylight and it doesn't shut down – you might have your eyes closed, but you're not properly resting. For fat-burning qualities, 4.00 a.m./5.00 a.m./6.00 a.m. are your best hours for actually burning body fat, so you're doing yourself a disservice by missing those in the stages of sleep in the circadian rhythm.

Sleep is probably one of the things that we don't really focus on because we've got the phone on all the time, the laptop on all the time, socialising quite late at night, and we work such long hours that by the time we get home we want to spend time with our loved ones, and before we know it's 1.00 a.m. and we're missing out on our sleep, which has such a knock-on effect within us.

EAT

Salt

Sodium is your secret weapon. Salt is your battery. If you don't have enough salt you're going to feel tired and flat. Your productivity, your mood and your sleep are all affected by salt. The reality is that when you eat clean you lose out on salts, because processed foods are very high in salt, so you need to increase your salt. Salt increases blood volume, which helps you with recovery. There is a small percentage of the population that is salt sensitive, just like those with peanut allergies, but in general sodium is your secret weapon.

The type of salt that will help you is iodised salt – it helps your thyroid, it stimulates your liver, it helps your metabolism and it really is the only detox that there is. The recommended daily intake for a normal, average person is 3-6 grams, but if you're an athlete or someone that trains and sweats a lot, then that would go up to 8 grams. Ideally salt should be taken with carbohydrates as that way it is pulled directly into the muscle and used efficiently.

Water

Now water is super important, but it's actually less important than sodium and less important than minerals, basically. The advice is to drink when you are thirsty. It's more important to focus on mineral intake rather than water intake. There is no set rule such as eight glasses, or three litres a day – that's BS. The problem is, if you are not having the right minerals then drinking lots of water is just basically flushing your system out even more, so it becomes detrimental to your health and fitness.

Protein

You *are* protein; you're made of protein. OK, you can get protein sources from other places, but you can't beat an animal protein to build an animal, which is scientifically proven. People struggle with knowing how much protein to ingest, but the recommended amount is one gram per pound of body weight. It's more important really how much you're getting *per meal*, so probably around 20 grams per meal for a normal person, or double that for an athlete. As you age you'll want to increase your protein intake, but never above 40 grams per meal.

You'll want to be eating protein four times a day, around every four hours or so.

BCAA (branched-chain amino acids) and glutamine are supplements that really aren't necessary and a waste of money, if you're having adequate protein with adequate meals in adequate timings then it's really not necessary for these things. They do have a place for people that have to be on low protein with their meals, but if you're on the correct amount of protein, and eating the correct amount of meals, then these things are of no value whatsoever. Once again it's just a product created by companies to market as necessary and generate more money. It's completely adequate to just eat foods as Mother Nature intended without clogging up your system and breaking the bank with all this other stuff that you just don't need.

And on that note, it's really beneficial for everyone to have a blood test every six months so that you can actually see what you need. You cannot guess what vitamins you need, or what your hormone situation is, so there is no point supplementing your diet with vitamins if they are not necessary.

Fats

Fats are *hugely* important. It's been proven in studies that the higher the fats in the diet, the lower the body fat. Fats can be found in our proteins and they manufacture our hormones. And if you're worried about cholesterol, it's actually genetic – so eating high fats isn't going to give you high cholesterol. If you're taking nutrients and vitamins and you're not taking in enough fats, then there is no way that the nutrient can get into the cell as they are shuttled into the cell through fats.

Normally, severe diets call for removal of all fats, all sugars and all fruit, but for females that's actually a really bad thing to do, as their upper body and lower body hold body fat in different ways, so if they have absolutely no fats in their diet they store fat on the lower part of their body. With each person the amount of fat to be included will differ, but it's important that they are in there.

Red meat

Andrea truly believes that red meat is really and truly the only wonder food on the planet. If there was nothing else in your diet but red meat, you would survive, and not just survive, you would thrive. If you can't afford steak then lamb is a good alternative.

Oils

All processed vegetable oils are poison; it's as simple as that. They create toxins, they are unstable and the body can't cope with them. Instead, just use animal proteins like steak, lamb, salmon, eggs, and vegetables as you can get all you need from them.

Carbs

Carbs are highly protective of muscle fibre, so if you are obese or insulin sensitive then you reduce the amount of carbohydrate, but if you are trying to build, grow and gain weight – *not fat,* gain weight – then you would increase them. It's just a simple case of managing your carbohydrates and choosing which ones are easier for you to digest – it's as simple as that.

Fructose

Fructose is necessary for the liver, and the liver is your body's chemist – it cleans out all the rubbish. You need fructose for the liver, but again, it's the amount; 75-100 grams of fructose is recommended per day, and this can quite easily be obtained through drinking orange juice each day.

TRAIN

Cardio

High impact cardio doesn't burn fat, it burns carbs. When people are dieting they tend to cut carbs from their diet, so when they then vigorously work out to burn fat what they are actually doing is depleting themselves. They are losing precious muscle fibre and exhausting themselves, which leads to adrenal problems and cortisol problems, which will cause lack of sleep, the gaining of body fat rather than dropping it, snappiness and moodiness with your loved ones, exhaustion, and it's basically just a vicious cycle that keeps spiralling out of control. So, cardio every now and then to increase fitness is fine, but high intensity cardio should not be used as a means of burning fat. When your heart rate is raised too high it stops your body from being able to supply fat for energy and therefore it is counterproductive as it just leaves you exhausted and tired, and then you will reach for food and the whole diet falls apart like a house of cards. So, for fat burn, choose slow and steady cardio (a brisk walk works absolutely fine), or some interval training with thirty seconds walk/thirty seconds light jog, on and off.

The amount of time to do that for will be dependent on your fitness level, age, weight and, of course, the overall goal.

REPEAT

Off the rails

If you 'fall off the wagon' or lose your way a little bit with your healthy eating and exercise regime, it's so important to not beat yourself up about it. You are human; give yourself a break – it's happened to all of us. Just relax, accept then let it go and regroup as soon as you can. There is no point grieving about it and using it as an excuse to not continue or to fall further off the wagon. Pick yourself up, dust yourself off and get back on your way. Remember to always think of where you are now in comparison to where you were when you first started, that's really important to do, as we so often lose sight of what we're achieving when we're living it each day. Logging things in diaries, and taking photos of your progress, are great ways to remind yourself of how far you have come and how well you have done.

Metabolic energy

When people want to get in shape and start dieting they put all their focus on losing weight, but that's not a true indication of anything, in fact, it can be a negative. What we need to do is try and get our heads around the fact that we need to *change our composition* rather than dropping weight on the scales. Yes, we want to drop fat but we also want to build muscle fibre. Now, you say this to some women and they freak out thinking that they're going to end up big and muscular – this is not true and this is not going to happen. Muscle is your help, muscle is your metabolic engine and muscle is what breaks calories down. So, all of the things that you do diet-wise and fitness-wise should be manufactured to support the breakdown of fat and the building of muscle fibre, rather than seeing a number drop on the scales and getting excited about it. Your excitement will be short-lived, as in order for the number to keep dropping on the scales, your muscle fibre will go and you will lose water. Yes, some fat will drop, but with every bit of muscle fibre that goes with it you set yourself back from your goal, because you've now lost the very thing that will help you burn fat and use up calories.

Juicing and fad diets do have their place for some people, but for most of the population, they do not. The aim is to generate muscle fibre and drop body fat, and do it in the safest way possible by not keeping yourself in a deficit with everything.

If you've ever been confused by the term 'skinny fat' then hopefully that makes sense to you now.

Nourish yourself and ensure you have enough minerals, enough water, enough sleep, enough exercise, enough rest and time to recover, and enough muscle fibre to use up any foods that you're putting in. Everything can be found from whole foods and Mother Nature, supplementation has a place for certain people and at certain times in your life, but on the whole it is not necessary.

PART 5

SELF-IMAGE

How you see yourself determines the success and failures in all aspects of your life. Your self-image is the foundation of your whole personality and it is the product of your past experiences. It's the picture you have created of yourself based upon your previous success and failures, humiliations and triumphs, and the way people have reacted to you in the past; it's a picture that you believe to be true. However, in many cases it is false.

If our mental image of ourselves is twisted then our reaction to our surroundings will be completely unrealistic.

The good news is, that you, and only you, created this mental picture in the first place so only you are capable of changing it and creating a new one, which puts all the power in your hands. By changing your mental picture, you can change your entire life along with it – there's no age limit as to when you can create a new self-image, and there's no cap on the amount of times you can do it either.

There's a lot of hype around positive thinking at the moment, and while this is definitely a tool to have in your life kit, it's not enough on its own. If your self-image is in tatters then positive thinking will only provide a crutch for it.

If you don't like yourself, then who will? How can you be positive about anything or anyone when you think so negatively of yourself? How can you truly love another if you do not love yourself? How can you see the beauty in things around you if you cannot see beauty within yourself? And it works both ways – if you see the love and beauty within you then you will see so much love and beauty outside of you, which obviously makes for a far happier, more peaceful and fulfilling life.

Your inner self-image mirrors your outer life experiences, so if we have a negative self-image we need to sort this out pronto! A negative self-image will cause our experiences in the real world to be just as negative and this gives our negative self-beliefs more anchorage, pulling us further away from positivity. It's a detrimental cycle that needs to be broken.

The pain-and-pleasure links from the previous chapter are the new ways of thought processing that need to be adopted to help tackle this along with the magical powers of your imagination. I shall explain...

IMAGINE THAT

There are not many things in life that are limitless, but your imagination is one of the very few, in fact, I'm actually struggling to think of anything else at all that has no bounds like the imagination does; and the truly awesome part? Every single one of us has one.

Remember how easy it was to completely lose yourself in a made-up reality as a child? Well, you still have that power, it's just that boring, 'grown-up' stuff got in the way like having to ensure you are liked by others to get ahead in life; in order to land good jobs, pay bills, etc. Basically, reality came down like a ton of bricks and burdened you with a lot of shit that (a) you weren't expecting and (b) then became too busy to deal with, which left you in a negative space with no time to dream up new realities and really focus on them, so that they could materialise. Your life as it is now did not just happen to you – you actually created it. You may not have consciously set out to create the life that you currently lead, but through your thoughts and beliefs you have shaped it to be the way it is today. Things don't happen to us, they happen *because* of us. Imagination and thinking creatively are such a powerful tools, and skills that some of us just don't use enough. We can change our entire outlook on life through our thought processes, and create new realities if we master it. Now this may all sound fluffy but there are case studies with athletes coming up to prove it. The brain is a physical thing that we know is there, but what about the mind? The mind has just as much reality as the brain even though we can't physically see it. Anyone who has ever felt happiness, or sadness, cannot question the presence of the mind. It thinks, it fears, it envisions and it's capable of taking a molehill... and creating a mountain.

Our imagination is the starting point for any goal we head for. Anything that we have pushed ourselves to achieve started out as a thought created by our imagination. The achievement of that goal is purely down to the fact that we kept the vision so vivid and alive in our minds, day in and day out, that it eventually became a reality. Your imagination is unbelievably powerful, and like most things in life you have a choice – you can use it for good, or you can use it for, well, the not so good. And when it comes to your imagination, the choice is 100% your own, it's yours and only yours after all.

Some of us have a terrible habit of assuming the worst. We lie awake at night feeling anxious through worry and stress about something we have to do the next day, and our imagination runs riot with all the ways it can go wrong. It's so powerful that it can think of literally *every* worst-case scenario, lump them all together and force you to envisage the following day as just one big fat disaster from start to finish. Watching the car crash of your day ahead so vividly in your mind is going to keep even the best sleepers wide awake at night. If you go into the next day with little or no sleep to function on, and with a one-track negative mindset, because you've built so much momentum with it that you then can't switch to the positive; it *will* end up a disaster.

But what if you tried the opposite approach? What if you imagined all the things that could go right, however far-fetched they seem, who cares? It's your imagination, no one is there to judge you on it. Well, as your imagination will spin off in whatever direction you point it in, you're going to be watching a very different movie as you lie there in your bed. The streets could be paved with gold while birds fly above, and you happily skip your way to the best job interview, or dinner date, of your entire life.

But we all hate disappointment don't we? During our early years we were conditioned by our elders to be prepared, which translates as 'expect the worst'. We get told by our parents: 'calm down,' 'take it easy,' 'be careful,' 'don't get too excited,' 'let's not count our chickens before they've hatched,' and so on, so forth, so it's no wonder that for a lot of us, our imagination has set itself to a negative default.

Worry is the most pointless thing one can do with the mind. It's a state of mind before the event has actually happened; it isn't real. Imagination isn't technically real either, but with the choice between the two, why waste your energy imagining a bad outcome when you can just as easily imagine a good one?

I can think of countless times that I've worried about something that has never happened, and in the few cases that one could argue that the worry was warranted, the worry in the lead-up was far more taxing on my emotional well-being than whatever actually happened.

The beautiful thing about our mind and our imagination is that they are ours, and only ours. We actually have full control over them. No one else programmes our minds but ourselves. Our imagination is ruled by our thoughts, and our thoughts are created based on past experiences, whether they are good, bad or neutral.

Here's a pretty awesome fact – the brain can't actually distinguish what is real from what is imaginary. I know, madness, right? But just think of all the power you have and the magic you can perform on yourself with this in mind – no pun intended, obviously.

Imagining and visualising ourselves functioning in a specific way is nearly the same as actual performance. Visualising a great performance before the real action is a popular training method used for the world's best athletes, as it mentally and physically prepares them for what is about to come. From physically stimulating the muscles necessary to perform the action, to the not-so-physical reframing of negative to positive outcomes in the mind for success.

For example, you may be familiar with the term, shadowboxing. Boxers use it to prepare the muscles and the mind by imagining an opponent in front of them and fighting them. This prepares them for the real fight, and there are plenty of studies out there to show that this method really works. Athletes have been hooked up to

EMG machines (machines that detect muscle activity) and the results show the exact same muscle activation on the ones who were imagining themselves performing their sport, as the ones who were actually, physically doing it.

Dr David Hamilton says:

> *It's pretty obvious when you think about it. The stress response evolved in humans to give us the ability to fight or flee when faced with danger. Chemicals including cortisol and adrenalin help kick-start the body, pushing blood towards the major muscles to give you strength. But the exact same stress response kicks in when you imagine danger, also producing cortisol and adrenalin and pushing blood around the body. The same chemistry is produced regardless of whether the danger is real or imagined.*
>
> *What does all this mean in real life? It means that what you imagine to be happening is actually happening as far as your brain is concerned.*[6]

Your imagination is literally your superpower, so let's see how we can use it for good, shall we?

When it comes to goals, we are in charge of our goals, no one else. Of course, outside things happen that we don't have control over and they can veer us off track, but we still have access to our imagination at all times to then creatively think of a solution to get us back on

---

6. *Dr David Hamilton <https://drdavidhamilton.com/does-your-brain-distinguish-real-from-imaginary>*

track again, or choose another pathway to get to our final destination.

If our minds control our actions, and our imaginations are used to dream up the goals towards which we head, there is absolutely no point in ever thinking negative thoughts at any time. This of course can be easier said than done. We can get caught off guard with devastating news, or things that trip us up in life, but so long as we pick ourselves up quickly, dust ourselves off and get back to a positive viewpoint, we can use our imagination to change our circumstances yet again. Along with exercising our imagination daily, it's this 'pick up, dust off' process that we also need to train ourselves to get good at.

Yes, it really is that easy, but unfortunately we don't help ourselves a lot of the time. As I explained in the compound effect previously, when we repeatedly make poor decisions we keep ourselves stuck on a negative track, which is super hard to get off, and then we spiral our way to bad outcomes. Along with our previous experiences that have formed our self-image and self-beliefs, we can also add insult to injury and strengthen our negative outlook and false beliefs about ourselves. We can continue to push down any glimpse of joy and deny positivity with our actions in many ways – we can watch the news and latch our focus on to the disasters it speaks of. We can block our minds consistently with mind-altering substances, such as sugar and alcohol. Or we can just hang around negative people who drip-feed us negativity through their conversation, and drain our energy as we try to push past the doom and gloom they speak of.

All of this stuff shapes our world and creates our reality, yet we still believe we are not in control of a lot of it. But we have a lot more control than we like to think we do, and we live in denial of this fact because our self-sabotaging actions provide us with instant gratification and other things we wouldn't be so forthcoming to admit. For example, hanging around negative people makes us feel superior and as if we are better, and more positive, people in the short term. The problem is in the long term; it weighs us down and makes us sell ourselves short in all areas of our life. Drinking alcohol and eating cake provides us with instant pleasure but affects our waistline as well as our mental capabilities, which allows us to achieve less in the long run by decreasing our mental and physical performance. At the end of the day we have choices all the time. We are responsible for the decisions that we make, and we then become the choices we make, so essentially, *we are our choices.*

But what if the right choice isn't obvious, you ask? It doesn't matter, because as long as you are keeping your side of the street clean so to speak, then you are using your imagination for good and are constantly creating, or strengthening, nothing but positive visions for your future. Doing this will automatically set you up to make the right choices – it won't even be a conscious decision on your part, which in itself makes life so much easier – who wouldn't rather have fewer decisions to make?

SELF-ACCEPTANCE

Working on a strong belief in yourself with your qualities and abilities is so important to carry forwards on the not-so-positive days when irritation crops up.

You are human; accept your limitations, please. Even an elastic band will break if you stretch it beyond its limits.

Mistakes happen, don't dwell on them, find the lesson and move on. There is no point torturing yourself with the past. Making mistakes is actually a great thing; it's the best way to grow and learn about ourselves and the world we live in – they are a positive not a negative.

Forgiveness is key – for yourself and for others. Holding grudges is negative and will get you nowhere. Holding a grudge with yourself is self-deprecating and holding grudges with others is negative and will affect your mindset and outlook on everything and everyone else.

We are our harshest critics, and our own worst enemies. Bad days happen. Fact. And there will be days that everything just looks or feels rubbish. It might be one bad event in your day that turns your outlook on everything within and around you, or you might just wake up in a not-so-favourable mood; you'll look in the mirror and struggle to find anything redeemable. These days happen, but they are just single days in the many days that we have, and it is a *temporary* state of mind that you're just going to have to ride out. Do not latch on to the negativity, just see it as it is, accept your mood, don't blame yourself or others for it and do not let your mind spin off with self-deprecating thoughts. Put your focus, and whatever energy you can muster up, into seeing your past successes and recapturing good feelings about yourself. It may seem difficult but I promise you that these bouts of depression and shitty moods are short-lived, and so long as you don't latch on to the negativity and allow them to spiral out of control and put you on a negative frequency for longer than necessary, then they will soon pass.

Personally, I find that sleep can solve a lot of things; I would describe it as a mind reset. Although I've tried many guided meditations, or just sitting there quietly, I'm rubbish at sitting still and meditating, so when my mind is whirring off on self-deprecation and I struggle to find good in anything around me, I simply take myself off for a nap. I just lie down quietly and accept that I'm 'in a mood' and let my body just relax. I'll naturally drift off and wake up about twenty to thirty minutes later feeling a little groggy at first, but within five minutes my mood and outlook has drastically improved and positivity begins to flow through me once again. Never underestimate the power of the nap, people!

As we grow up, part of the civilising process forces us to adopt masks to hide or modify our true feelings. The masks we wear serve to protect ourselves by hiding us from a threatening world. When we are children we express openly how we are feeling, but as we grow older we feel the need to put a brave face on, or bury ourselves under a façade to hide our vulnerability, as we don't want to be judged by others for appearing weak or small. While in some situations masks can help us push past our own limiting beliefs, get through a difficult day, or adapt ourselves to a new situation quickly and easily, they should only be used temporarily. We can sometimes get far too reliant on the use of masks – whether that's physical ones by hiding ourselves in the clothes we wear, or a full face of make-up, or the not-so-physical ones by constantly putting on a brave face and acting throughout our days.

By masking ourselves constantly we are denying our true selves and shattering our identities in the process, which creates poor self-image overall and has a negative impact on our self-beliefs. Constantly wearing a mask is seeking perfection at all times, which is exhausting and futile. You are human and so is everyone else. Perfection does not exist and you will have a far better time at genuinely connecting with the people around you if you take your mask off and simply be yourself, so that others feel at ease to be themselves too – it makes for a better world all round.

ADDICTED TO THE STRUGGLE

Relaxation is the first step to happiness. You cannot be happy if you are wound up like a clock spring and riddled with anxiety. You may think that by rushing around achieving goals you'll achieve the results that will make you happy in the long run, but this is untrue, and merely sets you up on the hamster wheel of exhaustion. You cannot relax and force yourself; the two simply don't go together.

By rationalising your on-the-go lifestyle of trying to better yourself, you are actually destroying yourself and blurring the lines of your self-image in the process. You won't even notice the 'better you' when you get there anyway, because when your mind and body can't take any more and you need to take a break, you'll bounce right back into self-loathing from sheer exhaustion, which will further support and strengthen your negative beliefs that you are a failure – and perhaps even unattractive with the signs of exhaustion on your body.

The problem with constantly striving for materialistic goals, be it new status, money or enhanced appearance, is that the work doesn't end with that single achievement; we have to then keep adapting ourselves to fit in with our new levels by gaining new airs of confidence and constantly striving for social acceptance. Constantly raising the bar higher and higher is exhausting, and not what life is about. If you dedicate all your time to this practice then you'll simply undo yourself in the process.

I believe a lot of us are addicted to the struggle. We push and push ourselves until we're all out of fight, and only when we are truly forced to stop and take some time out do we experience moments of true relaxation and happiness, which we then falsely associate with the strife and struggle that came before it. And so we enjoy our fleeting moments of time in relaxation and happiness with very short-lived feelings of accomplishment before angst sets in, and we start the whole process back up again a day or two later. I've been guilty of this in the past and it's no way to live a fulfilling life.

Most of us are carrying around a lot of grudges and angst, which fuel our fire to push ourselves further and further, but the problem with this is that the motivation is not coming from the self, it's coming from reactions to your past and you will never truly experience peace as long as you carry those grudges around with you. I've done this in the past and got pretty pro at using anger and grudges to boost me into action, and on paper have created much business success this way, but I have ended up resenting it in the long run because it didn't come from a place of love or happiness. I have created successes in the past purely from anger and lack of self-worth – I have behaved many a time like a woman possessed – but once out the other side with my so-called trophy or accomplishment, it does not feel like anything to celebrate and creates nothing but emptiness and the need to chase more out of further anger and even less self-worth... and so the cycle continues.

Call me crazy, but I'm pretty sure we were put on this earth to enjoy life and savour the calmness by interacting with all the beauty on this planet, not rush around it in panic and cloud our vision with countless anxieties.

Some of us have been doing this for so long that we've forgotten that there is any other way to live. Most of us will go to any lengths to avoid solitude, and we distract ourselves constantly with busy-ness or hanging out with the wrong people, and simply use their noise to deaden the noise of ourselves.

Most of us have been too busy to spend the time connecting with ourselves properly, which is why it's so awkward to sit down quietly and be one-on-one with ourselves. This is the first and foremost relationship that we should be concerning ourselves with – the relationship with ourself, as our self-image is the only one that can make us truly happy and create true success for us.

You may know some busy people who are killing it at life and look like they have their shit together, but more than likely they're just masters of the art of concealment. This is not only detrimental to one's health, but also pointless in the long run. As Ralph Waldo Emerson wrote: 'The civilised man has built a coach, but has lost the use of his feet'.[7]

---

7. Waldo Emerson, Ralph, *Self Reliance and Other Essays*

Anyhow, why spend so much time and energy mastering the art of concealment when you can master the relationship with yourself and in doing so hardwire yourself for automatic success in all areas no matter what the outside world throws at you?

BE YOURSELF; EVERYBODY ELSE IS TAKEN

The human race was not mass-produced. People are all different shapes and sizes and of different skin colour for a reason. We were never all meant to be the same, so it beggars belief why somewhere along the way we adopted this ridiculous idea that we should be like somebody else, or even everybody else.

One of my favourite quotes from Oscar Wilde, 'be yourself; everybody else is already taken' serves as a great reminder of the absurdity of trying to be like everybody else when everybody else is made of people of whom no two are the same.

You are you. I am me. No matter how hard I try, I will never be the same as anyone else on this planet, as I was never meant to be.

Uniqueness, which got a bit of a bad rap along the way as being labelled 'quirky', 'eccentric', 'different', sends our primitive brain into panic, which is the only reason I can think of that has us striving to imitate others and remain in the safe space of being like everybody else.

Let's get one thing straight – as a whole, each of us is neither inferior nor superior despite our negative self-talk telling us otherwise. I can't run as fast as Jessica Ennis-Hill. I can't match Serena Williams on the court. Further to that, I'm pretty sure you'd rather be watching Julia Roberts's acting skills play out on the movie you are enjoying, rather than viewing my attempt at a convincing performance. I meet people daily from accountants to sales reps to marketing managers, who are superior to me in some areas, but I don't compare myself to them, or beat myself up daily that I am inferior to them either. I doubt these people can draw, paint or apply make-up like I can, and there are other things that I'm better at too. And this is why we are completely wasting our entire lives by not capitalising on our God-given gifts and our own superior qualities, but instead concerning ourselves with inferiority to everybody else.

We were not created with a set of standards to conform to; everyone is made unique and individual. It's our birthright to own it - *all of it*. The fact that you are unique is the positive truth. The negative self-image of inferiority is the false one.

So please stop wasting your precious energy by putting your focus on things that aren't meant for you, and look right under your nose at all the awesomeness within you that you can nurture, grow and share with the world to make a difference that only you can, and create yourself one hell of a satisfying life.

You have an obligation to yourself to make life on this earth as happy as possible, so stop paying attention to all the wrong things and fighting it; you will never win because you can't be anything other than you. Be your friend, not your enemy.

It's not always easy but if you keep at it, and practise daily, then you will automatically change your self-image and make your life full of light, not full of darkness.

MIRROR IMAGE

Take a good hard look at yourself, and I mean *really* look at yourself in the mirror and identify your unique and positive qualities. This is where you want to focus – on the amazing uniqueness you already have. This is my main goal when working with my clients. It's far easier to build on what you already have than trying to change or acquire things that you don't already have. And within each of us is so much unique goodness that those around you love and would love to see more of. If you really can't see for yourself, please ask your friends, family, heck, ask the stranger on the street for the positive things they see in you. There are so many things, but you're too focussed on the things you don't like about yourself to notice the good. I see it all the time as my clients sit down in front of the mirror and immediately begin apologising for the way they look. I don't even notice these things until they point them out, and quite often I actually struggle to even identify with what they are saying as I can't see it. It's total madness and they are so fixated on the negative that they are completely blind to the positives, which there are always *far* more of. The negatives are completely unimportant in the grand scheme of things; they're just there – they shouldn't even be acknowledged, and *certainly* not at the expense of all the unique positives that should be thrust into the limelight, so that they can shine and not be hidden by a heavy fringe, or shaded and highlighted into something else.

Expending your energy on negative thoughts about parts of yourself that you don't like is a complete waste – it's far more productive and self-serving to put your focus into the things that you do like and nurture the crap out of those things, and those things only. We each have something (or rather some things – plural) special that is unique to us, and it's these unique qualities that we should be capitalising on, and truly owning, as they are ours and only ours. Our unique traits and physical features are things that no one can take away from us. We should take nothing but pride in the way we have been uniquely created and the individuality that is within us that sets us apart from everyone else. Before looking to change anything we should be accentuating our assets. When you learn to nurture and love the wonderful things that are already part of you, all the other stuff you're not so keen on will fade into the distance in comparison, and won't really matter anymore. Everything – strengths and flaws – becomes part and parcel of the whole of you; you'll realise you can't have one without the other. Your self-acceptance grows and with it your confidence and positivity about yourself grows too when you learn to love the unique things about you. We are all human, and living begins when we rise above our failures and shortcomings.

STINKING THINKING

Your false beliefs about your physical image can defeat your life goals. You must like and trust yourself before you can expect anyone else to like and trust you. If you're having to fake it all the time then you're going to assume everyone else is faking it too, and that will make for a very uneasy life having to second-guess everyone around you.

You need to get to know yourself, and know yourself well, so that your self-image is realistic and true to who you actually are and not built up of images of what you think other people want to see.

You are the master of your own ship and you must be your own compass in your mind. Looks aside, a lot of us kid ourselves and aim for what we think others want us to achieve rather than setting out for goals that mean something to us. It's often why we don't realise our successes, they were never ours to realise in the first place. We must be selecting goals that are *ours*. They need to be in line with our own skills and talents, and the tools available to us, so that they are realistic and easy to imagine into fruition.

It can be hard in today's world with so many ideals being thrown at us, but we need to stay true to who we are and not concern ourselves too much with others' ideals. As Martin Luther so eloquently put it: 'You cannot keep birds from flying over your head but you can keep them from building a nest in your hair.'

Like Dr Hanson earlier, I'm going to liken the mind to a garden – you can't plant cucumber seeds and expect to get tomatoes. The seeds you are planting in your mind with your imagination bear fruit of that which was planted. If you plant seeds of success then you will grow success, if you plant seeds of doubt and failure then you will grow negative experiences for yourself in your reality. It's your garden to grow whatever you want in, so make sure you're planting something good.

We can be so unkind to ourselves, far unkinder than we would ever dream of being to anyone else. When I'm feeling frustrated or angry with myself (or even anyone else for that matter) I think about a child. Would I be angry with a child for getting it wrong? Would I constantly be telling a child that their performance is poor? Would I be telling a child daily that they aren't good enough right now but they can be better? No, I would be nurturing that child, praising their achievements and lifting that child up daily, so that they had the power and confidence within themselves to be, and achieve, the great things that they are capable of. If you were verbally bashing a child on a daily basis it would be scared to do anything. That child would retreat and hide, with the negative words constantly reinforcing feelings of inadequacy and incapability. It's horrific to think that anyone would speak to a child this way, yet our own negative self-talk to ourselves can be very similar to this.

We need to increase our tolerance towards ourselves, have some patience and be kind. It's a daily practice and positive talk needs to be enforced daily. Sometimes we lose our temper, but we immediately feel guilty when we do as it's generally uncalled for, so forgive yourself if you lose your cool and just get yourself back to a positive mental attitude and reinforce your belief in your own capabilities with more conviction.

I'd like to wrap up this final chapter with a little exercise to help you rewrite any of your history that might be holding you back. I've kept physical exercises to a minimum as I wanted this book to serve more as a source of inspiration, and presentation of suggestions, rather than forcing you into doing some deep and time-consuming work right away, but this exercise is a powerful one, so don't skip it.

This method can be used over and over again, and as well as being used to reshape negative beliefs in the past, it can also be used to shape your future with things that are yet to happen.

With my passion for the arts, and as a lover of all things imaginative, I'd like you to create a cinema in your mind. You'll probably want to close your eyes for this, so read it first for the instructions, or record yourself speaking it and play it back when your eyes are closed.

> You're going to imagine that you are watching yourself on the big screen in the cinema.

Think back and find a memory that makes you feel sad or fearful, or any event in your memory that you feel negative towards. It could be a job interview, a task you failed at with work, rejection in any form from another person – perhaps someone made fun of you or your feelings of love were not reciprocated and you felt like a fool? It can be anything at all. Conjure up the past situation in your mind and make it strong so that you can clearly see it, and feel it, and then rate the level of negative emotion it brings up in you from 1 to 10.

Now that you're fully in that feeling, and you've rated it on a scale of 1 to 10, you're going to remove the image from your mind and create a new one.

This time, before thinking of anything else, I want you to think of what you want in life. What you truly want. And picture yourself, as you'd truly like yourself to be. Once you've given that some thought, visualise you as this person and project your new self-image onto the big screen in front of you.

Now you're going to use your imagination to create the same scene as before, but with a different outcome – a far more favourable and positive one.

You're going to imagine every detail in relation to the situation. The place you were in, your surroundings, the colour and details of the things around you, and you're going to see it on the screen in front of you, and with your new self-image you're going to walk into the same negative situation you imagined previously only this time you're going to watch it play out in the opposite way.

Just like when we get taken in by watching movies with great actors and realistic effects, you're going to create a very real image on the screen in front of you. You're going to feel the positive energy surrounding the image of you on this big screen. You're going to watch yourself on the big screen, standing tall, looking assured and you're going to watch the scenario play out in a positive way. You're going to see yourself really engaging with the space in a positive way through your body language, your speech and through the reactions of others that are there with you, and you'll see yourself connecting with the person or task in a way that there is no alternative but for a positive outcome. Make this image super strong and really feel all the goodness and positive sensations that this picture is bringing up within you.

Act out the whole scene from start to finish like before, and really immerse yourself in it – see it and feel it, as if it were real.

Then open your eyes.

Now think back to that negative memory again; is there less sadness or fear attached to it? Perhaps you feel completely indifferent to it, like it never happened at all? Rate the feelings of negativity you have towards it on a scale of 1 to 10. The number should have gone down, but if you still have some uncomfortable feelings towards it then you can repeat the exercise and disassociate more and more negativity with it each time until you eventually get a 0 on the negative emotion scale.

The mind is really the most powerful tool we have. But, if we don't keep it in check it can have us play out our lives in misery while it holds on to negative things that either happened to us, or that were said to us in our past, and then use them to create fear to keep us safe from similar occurrences in the future. Negative emotions get stored in our minds and manifest in all parts of our bodies, but they are false, they have no place or purpose. They are simply events that have passed, they should have no emotion attached to them as they are no longer real – they have been and gone and are simply a memory. There is no need to continue feeling bad about something that happened in the past, it serves no purpose. The past cannot be changed, and there are plenty of new opportunities for positivity in our now, and in our future. So, check in with yourself every now and again. Just like you do a desktop clean-up on your computer every so often, you should be doing the same with yourself by scanning your body, and your mind, to ensure that no rubbish is being stored that is slowing you down. Even if you don't regularly 'scan' for these things, just be aware and notice when something comes up and it induces a strong feeling within you – question the origin of that feeling to decipher whether it's true or not, and perform the previous exercise on it to change your feelings towards it so that you loosen its hold on you.

FINAL WORD

We're approaching the final pages of the book, and haven't we covered some ground?

You know, I mapped out this book as best I could, but I knew it would change as I started writing it, and sure enough it did. My spreadsheet of book structure and chapter organisation has changed more times than I care to remember. I worried I was going off on tangents on many occasions, but uncovering the surface, removing the filter and going beneath the superficial was necessary. We should be approaching the exploration of our internal make-up wide eyed and with just as much wonder and excitement as we approach the beauty counter. All the products we will ever need are within us.

I was told a book needed to be 'this and that' before and during writing these pages, but I held my self-belief strong and just wrote what I felt to write, feeling secure in knowing that it would come good in the end – it had to.

I personally felt that the world didn't need another book about make-up techniques, products or trends, I felt we didn't need another book to tell us how we should look or how we should behave. While I love the work that I do, and I love the magic I can perform through make-up artistry, I felt I had a lot more in my heart and head to offer than just that, and there were just too many things that have helped me over the years to keep bottled up and not share with you, as you may just find them helpful too.

I wanted to create a book that planted some seeds, that simply suggested some ideas and started a conversation within whoever read it. It's always good to talk, especially with ourselves – just like we learn about others by asking questions, we learn so much about ourselves through asking questions too. Each one of us is fascinating, even to ourselves, so take interest. We think we know ourselves, but we've all got some surprises within us if we dig deep – and the path of self-discovery is one that we should be choosing each day.

There's so much to learn about our own identity, and the individuality within us, that can't be taught but only felt, discovered and realised. It's not a boring class we must take to learn, it's a journey, and there is much joy to be had in the adventure of this journey if you just lean into it and keep your mind open.

If we think ourselves into ugliness we can think ourselves into beauty. If we can bring a bad day upon ourselves then we can just as easily bring many more days of happiness. We are in charge. We have ourselves, we always will, and no one can take us away from us. We can choose to see what we want to see within ourselves, and within everything that surrounds us.

We really do create our own reality, and our reality is the only one that matters. It can be made up of our own opinions, or it can be made up of others' opinions – you get to decide.

Remember, we can't move forward with one foot in the past. Sure, it can be hard to make changes, and there is comfort in staying the same place, but there is so much fun to be had on the other side if we just take some chances and move past our fears.

Old habits can die hard, we have so much memory in our bodies, from muscle memory to our actual memory. Having lived a certain way for so long it can be all too easy to fall back into old beliefs and negative thinking, but that's OK, and it will happen every now and again. We're all human and perfection does not exist, nor should it as that would make for a pretty boring life for us all. When you stumble just pick yourself up, and remember that the power of change is in your hands, and no one else's. You can get yourself back on track with the tools in this book, you can remind yourself of what is really going on, and you have your wonderful imaginative abilities to dream up and create new realities whenever you need them.

You are the longest relationship you will ever have, so invest time in it, make sure it's the best relationship of your life – be kind to yourself, get to know yourself and be your best friend.

As a thank you for taking a chance on me and picking up this book, I have some gifts for you to help you on your way to being the best version of yourself, your very best version yet.

Head over to: www.camillacollins.com/nofilterneeded to gain access to them.

Once again, thank you. I really hope you got something out of these pages and if there's anything you want to chat about or have any questions relating to the topics covered in this book then please do reach out to me via my website www.camillacollins.com or on social media.

 I hold many quotes in my mind but time and time again, with almost everything I do and every time I embark on something new or uncomfortable, I remind myself "Start where you are. Use what you have. Do what you can."

FURTHER READING

Hardy, Darren, *The Compound Effect* (New York: Carroll & Graf, 2012)

Erod, Hal, *The Miracle Morning* (London: John Murray Learning, 2017)

Maltz, Maxwell, *Psycho-Cybernetics* (London: Perigee, 2015)

Maltz, Maxwell, *The Magic Power of Self-Image Psychology* (London: Simon & Schuster, 2008)

Peters, Prof. Steve, *The Chimp Paradox* (London: Vermilion, 2012)

Robins, Mel, *The 5 Second Rule* (Brentwood: Post Hill Press, 2017)

Schwartz, David, *The Magic of Thinking Big* (London: Vermilion, 2016)

Sincero, Jen, *You are a Badass* (London: John Murray Learning, 2016)

Tracy, Brian, *Eat That Frog* (New York: McGraw-Hill Education, 2017)

Forleo, Marie, Everything is Figureoutable (Penguin 2019)

REFERENCES

https://en.wikipedia.org/wiki/History_of_cosmetics

https://www.fda.gov/cosmetics

Mintel Press Office: https://www.mintel.com/press-centre/beauty-and-personal-care/all-polished-up-nail-make-up-steals-the-show-in-uk-cosmetics-market

Dr Rick Hanson, THE BRAIN https://s3.amazonaws.com/nicabm-stealthseminar/Brain2017/NICABM-Brain-Infographic.pdf

Dr Rick Hanson in West Wight Sangha Audio http://west-wight-sangha-audio.blogspot.com/2014/10/pet-lizard-feed-mouse-hug-monkey-by.html

https://www.mentalhealth.org.uk/sites/default/files/DqVNbWRVvpAPQzw.pdf

https://en.wikipedia.org/wiki/Lipstick_effect

http://beautyandthebullshit.blogspot.com

Dr David Hamilton <https://drdavidhamilton.com/ does-your-brain-distinguish-real-from-imaginary>

Waldo Emerson, Ralph, *Self Reliance and Other Essays*

ACKNOWLEDGEMENTS

First and foremost I'd like to thank the wonderful humans who were so open and generous in sharing their professional and personal stories: Rowena, Zoe, Sarah, Paula, Andrea, Laura and Janette; a big thank you for helping me add so much value to these pages and making this book as comprehensive as it is.

A huge thank you to every single one of my wonderful clients who have supported and allowed me to practice my craft over the last decade and have shared so much of themselves with me and helped me grow both professionally and personally.

To my long suffering parents, Ashley and John, thank you for standing by me through the many highs and lows of the last 32 years. I am eternally grateful to your constant love and support and for picking me up every time I fall - you both have a ridiculous amount of patience and truly deserve a medal!

And to all my friends, in both a personal and professional capacity, you continue to spur me on and lift me up each day - your support means the world to me and I wouldn't be pushing out of my comfort zone as much (or as hard) as I do without knowing you lovely lot have got my back! And please know that I will always have yours.

CONTACT CAMILLA

www.camillacollins.com

www.instagram.com/camillajcollins

www.facebook.com/camillajcollins

www.linkedin.com/in/camillajcollins

www.twitter.com/camillajcollins

NOTES

Following are a few pages for you to write your thoughts.